BEHIND THE FAÇADE
OF STALIN'S
COMMAND
ECONOMY

BEHIND THE FAÇADE OF STALIN'S COMMAND ECONOMY

EVIDENCE FROM THE SOVIET STATE AND PARTY ARCHIVES

Paul R. Gregory

EDITOR

HOOVER INSTITUTION PRESS
STANFORD UNIVERSITY
STANFORD, CALIFORNIA

Hoover Institution Press Publication No. 493

First printing 2001
Manufactured in the United States of America

06 05 04 03 02 01   9 8 7 6 5 4 3 2 1

The paper used in this publication meets the minimum requirements of American National Standard for Information Sciences—Permanence of Paper for Printed Library Materials, ANSI Z39.48-1984. ♾

Library of Congress Cataloging-in-Publication Data

Behind the façade of Stalin's command economy : evidence from the Soviet State and Party archives / Paul R. Gregory, editor.
    p. cm.
    Includes bibliographical references and index.
    ISBN 0-8179-2812-X (alk. paper)
   1. Soviet Union—Economic policy. 2. Soviet Union—History—1925–1953. 3. Stalin, Joseph, 1879–1953. I. Gregory, Paul R.

HC335.3 .B44 2001
338.947—dc21   2001024459

CONTENTS

PREFACE

The opening of the formerly secret Soviet state and party archives in the early 1990s was an event of profound significance. Western scholars, who previously used Kremlinology to penetrate the official wall of secrecy, could now use the same documents as had Soviet leaders in earlier periods. The Soviet state and party archives have already permitted historians to rewrite the political history of the USSR. Few deep secrets remain, especially concerning the 1920s and 1930s. Economists—relative latecomers to the use of these archives—can now use them to study the still poorly understood workings of the Stalinist command economy. Although the Soviet command economy is supposedly a thing of the past, it continues to plague Russia's transition to a market economy, and, more important, it continues to have considerable emotional appeal as a substitute for a market economy. Voices are already being raised claiming that the Soviet command economy was sound but it was run by the wrong people, who made wrong decisions. The archives give us a real opportunity to examine such propositions.

This book summarizes economic research based on the Soviet state and party archives. It brings together prominent scholars from Russia, the United States, and the United Kingdom, many of whom have worked with these archives since they were opened. Topics are discussed in this collection—the economics of the

Gulag, the management of military innovation, the specifics of defense budgets, Stalin's handwritten marginal comments on planning documents, internal Politburo discussions—the coverage of which could not have been imagined twenty years ago. Each chapter focuses on what we have learned from the archives, on what has surprised us and what has simply confirmed what we already knew. These essays cover the period from the early 1930s through Stalin's death in 1953, namely, the period of creating the Stalinist system. Since for the postwar era Soviet state and party archives remain basically closed, archive-based research on the "mature" Soviet economy will have to be done by future researchers.

This publication had its origins in discussions with John Raisian, director of the Hoover Institution on War, Revolution and Peace, and with Charles Palm, deputy director, in the summer of 1998 concerning the need to bring to the attention of general readers the results of ongoing archive-based research on the Soviet command system. As the result of a series of agreements with the State Archival Service of Russia beginning in 1992, the Hoover Institution has acquired almost ten thousand microfilm reels of the files of the Soviet Communist Party and state. Because of the deteriorating physical condition of these archives in Russia and the uncertainty of future access, the presence of these archives in Hoover ensures that scholars can mine this treasure of information over many decades.

I am particularly grateful for the support of the Hoover Institution of this project, one product of which is the publication of this book. The chapters by myself, Eugenia Belova, and Aleksei Tikhonov are the products of research conducted in the Hoover Archives and, together with the other chapters of the book, were supported financially by the Hoover Institution through a generous gift of the Lakeside Foundation. I would particularly like to thank John Raisian and Charles Palm for their appreciation of and support of this work. We would also like to thank the dedicated staff of the Hoover archives as a whole but would wish to single out Charles Palm, Elena Danielson, and Lora Soroka, without whose assistance this project could not have been carried out. A final word of thanks goes to Patricia Baker, executive editor of the Hoover Press, who sure-handedly navigated this volume to completion in spite of the difficulties of dealing with authors widely dispersed across the globe.

PAUL R. GREGORY

References to archival material are given using original notations—fond (f.), opis (op.), delo (d.), and list (l.)—accepted in Russian archives.

CONTRIBUTORS

EUGENIA BELOVA is a Ph.D. candidate in economics, University of Houston, and is currently a visiting fellow at the Hoover Institution.

JOSEPH S. BERLINER is Professor Emeritus at Brandeis University and Senior Associate at the Davis Center for Russian Studies, Harvard University.

R. W. DAVIES is Professor Emeritus at Birmingham University and former Director of its Centre for Russian and East European Studies.

PAUL R. GREGORY is a Distinguished Visiting Fellow at the Hoover Institution and is the Cullen Chair of Economics at the University of Houston.

MARK HARRISON is Professor of Economics at Warwick University.

OLEG KHLEVNYUK is Senior Researcher at the Russian State Archival Service.

E. A. REES is Professor of History at the European University Institute, Florence, Italy.

ALEKSEI TIKHONOV is a former scientific researcher, Department of History, Moscow State University, and is currently a visiting fellow at the Hoover Institution.

1 | THE CONTRIBUTION OF THE SOVIET ARCHIVES

Joseph S. Berliner

This book addresses the economic history of the Soviet Union under Stalin from the vantage point of the recently opened Soviet state and party archives. Although considerable archive-based research on that period has been published over the past five years, relatively little work has been devoted to the economics of the Stalin system. The authors of the chapters that follow pose a common question: What can we learn about the Stalinist command system from these formerly secret official archives that we could not have learned prior to their opening? It is therefore appropriate for me to explain how pioneering researchers began to study the Soviet economic system after World War II, before turning to a discussion of new insights provided by the archives.

Students of the Soviet society under Stalin operated under restrictions that were far in excess of those encountered in the study of any other modern society. They had no direct access to the country and its citizens, for only people like diplomats and journalists could receive permission to reside there. Since they could not tap directly into the knowledge and opinions of Soviet citizens, they had to rely on whatever information they could glean from publications that the government permitted to be exported—publications which, of course, were subjected to strict censorship, and therefore possibly inaccurate or incomplete.

Occasionally the veil was lifted by the accounts of former diplomats and journalists, of visiting delegations of foreign observers, and of defectors. A further unusual source of information came from the large number of former Soviet citizens stranded in Western Europe after World War II—Soviet army deserters, forced laborers in German factories, or collaborators who had retreated with the German occupiers. Interviews with these people provided the only large-scale data set on the life experiences and attitudes of people who had actually lived in the Soviet regime.[1] For the rest, students of the USSR felt somewhat like historians of ancient societies, fated never to see the country whose history and life they tried to piece together from the scraps that had escaped the ravages of time.

One was able, then, to read many of the newspapers and books that Soviet people read and to see many of the films that Soviet people saw. What one missed were the books and articles that would have been written by Soviet people had they been free to offer their views and to describe and to criticize their world in the manner of writers in "normal" countries. Imagine trying to understand the British or the Mexicans if one had no access to the views of citizens who saw their country differently from the way their government wished them and the world to see it.

There were, however, several sources of insight into the society that the censors did not seek to suppress. Some of the meetings of the Supreme Soviet and the Communist Party, for example, were public events to which foreign diplomats and some journalists were invited. These meetings were the occasion for formal reports by such government officials as the prime minister, the foreign minister, the minister of finance, and the chairman of the State Planning Commission. Their reports provided varying amounts of selected information on the organization of government, on who was appointed to what position, on the progress of

---

1. Alex Inkeles and Raymond Bauer, *The Soviet Citizen* (Cambridge, Mass.: Harvard University Press, 1959); Joseph Berliner, *Factory and Manager in the USSR* (Cambridge, Mass.: Harvard University Press, 1957).

government policies new and old, and on foreign policy developments. Because the formal proceedings of such meetings were published, their accumulation over the years provided a considerable body of information about the state of the economy and of political affairs that became an important data base for scholars. It was a small thing compared with the thick statistical abstracts, white papers, and other government reports of other countries, but it was something.

A second valuable body of material consisted of publications that the government accepted as necessary for the effective functioning of the society. The large educational establishment, for example, had to have textbooks that instructed students in how government and economy functioned. Economists and political analysts had to be permitted to publish the results of their research on issues of the day, and scientists, agronomists, and engineers had to communicate with their colleagues and inform their readership of advances in their fields. Though heavily censored to protect national security and suppress dissident views, Soviet publications of these sorts provided an important flow of information that was useful for the work of scholars abroad.

The third source of information, and the most distinctively Soviet, was the literature of so-called *samokritika*, or "self-criticism." It derived from Lenin's insightful concern that under conditions of full employment and job security, and in the absence of the profit motive, managers and workers might be increasingly inclined to feather their own nests, to "sit on their hands," and to live an easy life, rather than put in a full day's work as they had to do under capitalism. The best answer Lenin could come up with was to enlist the press and the whole society in a permanent campaign to expose and root out such instances of self-seeking and antisocial behavior. The consequence was that the Soviet press often featured articles that revealed many of the malfunctions and tensions within the system. A disgruntled engineer might criticize his factory director for deliberately omitting some stages in the production process that made it possible to increase the rate of output but at the expense of lower quality of goods. A local planning-board official might report that several enterprises continued to spend lavish sums on "expediters" who were sent to their supplier-factories with gifts and bribes to ensure that they received their supplies of fuels or materials on time. Such articles transformed the reading of newspapers with such unpromising titles as "For Industrialization" and "The Construction Gazette" into mines of information that might yield nuggets of gold if you worked at them long enough. They provided a certain voyeuristic thrill, like peeking into the seamy sides of a society whose government wished you not to know about.

It was evident that one had to be cautious in drawing inferences from materials of these sorts; perhaps an article may not have been written by the reported author but had been planted there by the editor to serve his own or the Party's purpose. In the course of time, however, a lore accumulated on how to read between the lines of the Soviet press and on what pitfalls to anticipate. Initiation into that lore was part of the training of new students by their teachers.

Since Western accounts of Soviet society relied so heavily on published Soviet sources, a crucial question for the research community was the degree of confidence one could place in those materials. If the sources reported that 16.3 million tons of steel were produced in 1938 or that the average monthly wage was 33.1 rubles, could one use those figures with confidence in estimates of national product or levels of living? The question was widely discussed in the early postwar years, and in the course of time most scholars came to believe that the use of information for political and propaganda purposes took the form primarily of suppression, rather than outright falsification. For example, in a year when the harvest was poor, the size of the harvest would simply not be reported. One could, in fact, often infer poor results from the omission of a statistic that was normally reported.

Two pieces of evidence may be cited for the view that published data were generally usable. One was the famous 1941 Plan.

In the late 1930s the government ceased publishing its annual economic plans. It was the custom, however, for the chairman of the State Planning Commission to give the Supreme Soviet a report on the plan for the forthcoming year, which was then published in the major newspapers. The statistics presented in these reports were a primary source of information on the performance of the economy. If they were falsified, much foreign research on the USSR would have been worthless.

As it happened, when the Germans invaded the USSR in June 1941, they scooped up a large volume of documents that had been left behind by fleeing Soviet citizens—perhaps the first opening of the Soviet archives. The documents were found in Germany by Allied troops after the war, and among them was a copy of the National Economic Plan for 1941. Each page of it bore the legend, "Not for Circulation." Examination of this document showed that the statistics publicly reported by the planning chairman in his report were virtually identical to those contained in the secret plan. It was evident that the published figures were those that Soviet officials themselves used in planning the economy. The incident greatly increased the confidence of analysts that published data could generally be used to analyze Soviet economic performance.

One could not always be sure, however, and various techniques were developed to test the validity of data, such as tests for consistency. An analyst of the construction industry, for example, noticed that in a certain year, financial expenditures on housing construction declined, but the quantity of new housing put in place increased. She also noticed what appeared to be a change in terminology; the report referred to "total floor space," instead of "dwelling floor space" as in the past. A technical encyclopedia eventually confirmed her suspicion: total floor space included hallways and stairwells, which dwelling floor space excludes. It was evident that whoever reported the figures wanted to give the impression that housing construction had increased by using a different measure of housing, and without disclosing the fact to the reader. In an important footnote to the story, the researcher discovered that total floor space is almost invariably about 30 percent larger than dwelling floor space, which enabled her to recalculate the data so as to obtain a consistent time series. The lesson of this and similar incidents is that one had to be on guard against individual acts of deception, but when the deception was discovered, the underlying numbers were generally accurate enough to reveal the truth.

Although the weight of evidence supported the view that the published data could be used to provide a reasonably accurate picture of the society, there always remained the slight nagging possibility that that confidence was misplaced and that we had been taken in by Soviet propaganda. Hence the opening of the Soviet state and party archives was greeted with some excitement. At last there was an opportunity to tell whether we had got it right or whether we were way off base.

This volume is a contribution to a rapidly growing body of research using materials from the newly opened Soviet archives. As several of the authors note, this research is only at its beginning and an enormous volume of material remains to be analyzed— more than enough for a generation of scholars. For example, as Davies notes, the number of published decrees of the Council of People's Commissars amounted to only about one-tenth of the total number of decrees issued in the 1930s; the unpublished decrees resided in the archives all these years and are now available for study. It is now possible to write detailed histories of policies and institutions in a degree of detail that could not be achieved before.

Although the research published thus far has "done no more than sample" the archives (Harrison), some broad generalizations may be made on the contribution of archival research. Perhaps the most significant generalization is that the Soviet Union one sees in the archives is perfectly recognizable to people who have tried to understand it through the open sources alone. The investigators of the Party Control Commission focus on the same problems that had been identified earlier by analysts of the published sources—falsification of information by managers, bribery and corruption, and so forth (Belova). In this respect the archives provide confirmation that Western research had got it largely right.

The contribution of the archives to the advancement of understanding varies from one level of society to another. It is smallest in the case of primary organizations such as enterprises, farms, schools, and hospitals. The materials collected by the inspectors of the Party Control Commission, for example, confirm the extent to which enterprises engaged in illicit behavior of various sorts. There were some practices, however, that were not detected in the published sources but are revealed in the Party Control Commission archives, such as the extent to which files disappeared from local party and government offices, and the prevalence of illegal sales and speculation in party membership cards (Belova).

The "value added" by the archives is greater in the case of the higher administrative organizations like the ministries and the State Planning Commission. From the available information, one could paint a broad picture of how they were organized and how they operated, but most of what one learned about them came from accounts of enterprise dealings with them—that is, from the enterprise perspective. Now these organizations are no longer shrouded in mystery, for the archives are overflowing with reports, decrees, and correspondence at this level of the society. The chapter by Tikhonov and Gregory, for example, reveals the intense infighting among the State Planning Commission, the State Supply Committee, and the Ministry of Finance over drafts of the Fifth Five-Year Plan—none of which appeared in the press.

It was at the very top of the level of power that the open sources provided the least information. How the Politburo and the Party Central Committee were organized, how they carried out their work, and the role of Stalin in their activities, was a virtual void, except for bits and pieces found in occasional memoirs, many of them by foreigners who had top-level access from time to time. The archives provide an exhilarating view of the activities at this level. Reading Stalin's marginal notes on a report by Molotov, one is without doubt seeing the system at work. Particularly striking is the arbitrariness with which major decisions were made. Stalin, for example, repeatedly interfered with the planning process, raising or reducing investment targets by large amounts with no apparent economic justification (Davies; Gregory). On the other hand, he was generally well informed (Rees) and he did listen to different opinions, and was sometimes influenced by them; he greatly scaled down the size of planned grain collection in 1932 after hearing the reports from the localities on how severe the consequences would be (Davies). The casualness with which important decisions were made provides strong evidence for Eugène Zaleski's conclusion that the Soviet economy should be regarded as "managed" rather than "planned."[2] These archives are of greatest use to political historians who, in the past, had to figure things out from open sources alone. Such histories can now be based on archival sources.[3]

The archival material tends to generate a certain sympathy for the plight of the State Planning Commission. On the one hand they were subject to arbitrary changes in their plans by Stalin, either on his own account or in response to the numerous appeals by commissars to change planners' decisions. On the other hand, they worked with an exceedingly small staff, consisting of only 900 people in the early 1930s (Gregory). The archives thus throw a new light on the State Planning Commission and its performance; much of what appeared to be inefficiency should perhaps be ascribed to an overload of work and an undersupply of staff.

The archives also present a rather different picture of the nature of the control exercised by and within the top leadership. From the history of purges and dismissals of ministers and planning officials it had been evident that there were periods of sharp

2. Eugène Zaleski, *Stalinist Planning for Economic Growth, 1933–1952* (Chapel Hill: University of North Carolina Press, 1980).

3. O. V. Khlevnyuk, *Politburo: Mekhanizmy politicheskoi vlasti v 1930-e gody* (Moscow: Rosspen, 1996).

conflict among the top leadership. The archives now make it clear that the source of the conflict was the extreme difficulty for senior officials, starting with Stalin, to maintain control over their juniors. The Politburo feared disloyal technicians in the State Planning Commission (Gregory), the Party Control Commission had to punish corrupt judges and local party officials (Belova), industrial ministers who were also Politburo members pursued their own agendas (Gregory), and local party officials defied Politburo orders (Belova). Differences in objectives within the center suggest an extremely complex system that was difficult to manage.

The contribution of the archives varies not only by level of power but also by sector of the society. It is greatest in the case of those sectors about which the government had been most secretive, such as the security apparatus, the Gulag, and the military. The archives bearing on these sectors provide a picture of how they operated that could not have been put together on the basis of the published sources alone—for example, Khlevnyuk's detailed account of the scale of labor-camp operations. His evidence confirms the view that political and not economic motives dominated in the decision to build the Gulag, and that the camps were in fact grossly inefficient. With regard to the military, the published sources gave virtually no information about the activities of defense contractors. The archives, however, made it possible for Harrison to study them in depth. He finds, among other things, that defense contractors acted much like civilian managers, concealing costs, raising prices when they could, and withholding information from the military.

In general, the value of the archives is that they make it possible to fill in much of the detail regarding policies and organization that was previously unknown. They offer glimpses of things that were not brought to light at the time, such as the "strong impetus to reform" manifested in the steady stream of reformist proposals from the staff of the Commissariat of Finance and other agencies urging a greater role for prices and profits (Davies). And they provide information that helps to settle issues that in the past could be no more than surmises. For example, it had been charged the USSR falsified and understated its published military budgets in 1931–1933 in order to influence the Geneva disarmament negotiations (Harrison, citing Davies). The material in the archives makes it possible to reconstruct defense expenditures at that time, and it turns out that the charge was valid. What was formerly a surmise can now be taken as fact. On the other hand, some surmises turn out to have been incorrect: For example, Stalin was not a nonentity in 1920s at the time of Lenin's death but was already a favorite of those in the know (Rees). Nor can the view be sustained that the Politburo was divided into moderates and hardliners; the whole leadership varied from moderate to hard-line policies according to the issues. Nor is there any evidence of Stalin's involvement in Kirov's assassination (Rees). Also, the Soviet military was much stronger in 1941 than was sometimes supposed; if not for secrecy, the Germans might have known the true Soviet strength and might not have attacked (Harrison, citing Samuelson).

In conclusion, the archives have confirmed that the sources available to foreign scholars in the past, though not abundant and heavily censored, enabled them to draw a fairly accurate picture of the USSR in Stalin's time. As Davies writes, "The new information has not brought about a revolution in our understanding of the Soviet economic system." But our understanding is now, because of the archives, much more complete, detailed, and nuanced. One waits with anticipation the further new insights that may be expected when scholars get beyond the "first sampling" phase of archival research, which the following chapters describe.

2 THE DICTATOR'S ORDERS

Paul R. Gregory

The Soviet administrative-command economy was the most important socioeconomic experiment of this century. It was formed without a theoretical blueprint, the product of trial-and-error and of initial conditions. Beginning in 1928 and 1929, Stalin and his allies embarked on a course of rapid industrialization and forced collectivization, which required the creation of a new command economic system. The Soviet leadership had fashioned, by the mid-1930s, an economy of full state ownership with resource allocation managed through administrative balances of material, labor, and financial resources. Planning was carried out by the State Planning Commission (Gosplan) and the Ministry of Finance, but operational resource allocation was the responsibility of industrial ministries, which managed state enterprises and collective farms. The Soviet "state" was a close amalgam of the Politburo of the Communist Party and the Council of Ministers (then called the Council of People's Commissariats, called Sovnarkom). These organizations are described in detail in the chapter by Rees. This system remained remarkably unchanged until its collapse at the end of 1991.

If the book were closed on the Soviet system today, some

The author would like to thank the Hoover Institution and the National Science Foundation for their support of this research.

would contend that it was doomed from the start by the systemic problems outlined by Mises and Hayek in their classic critique of planned socialism written in the 1920s and 1930s. Others would argue that the Soviet system, which transformed Russia from backwardness to industrial power, failed because of inept policies and incompetent administrators, not because of the system itself. The recent opening of the Soviet state and party archives provides an opportunity to determine who was to blame—people and policies, or the system itself? The chapters in this collection all address this issue, either directly or indirectly, using the (mostly secret) documents from the Soviet state and party archives that Soviet decision makers themselves used.

PLANNERS' PREFERENCES

Abram Bergson introduced the term "planners' preferences"—the notion that the Soviet administrative-command economy was ultimately directed by the top leadership of the Communist Party, unlike market economies, which are ultimately directed by consumer sovereignty.[1] Planners' preferences were expressed principally as *plans* (for outputs, inputs, investments, labor staffing, and cost reductions), drawn up according to the directives of the Soviet dictatorship. This chapter studies how the dictator's preferences were used to shape the economy according to the dictator's will. We know that these preferences mattered. We have conclusive evidence that the command system yielded economic outcomes quite different from a market economy.[2] Soviet-style economies produced more heavy industry and defense goods and fewer services, and had higher investment rates and lower rates of urbanization than market economies at a similar level of eco-

1. Abram Bergson, *The Real National Income of Soviet Russia Since 1928* (Cambridge, Mass.: Harvard University Press, 1961).
2. Gur Ofer, *The Service Sector in Soviet Economic Growth* (Cambridge, Mass.: Harvard University Press, 1973); Simon Kuznets, "A Comparative Appraisal," in Abram Bergson and Simon Kuznets, eds., *Economic Trends in the Soviet Union* (Cambridge, Mass.: Harvard University Press, 1963).

nomic development. Moreover, Soviet planned economies devoted more resources to agriculture and relied less on foreign trade.

COMMANDING HEIGHTS AND SMALL STAFFS

The Soviet "dictator" was the Politburo, which consisted of about ten of the Soviet Union's top Party leaders headed by Joseph Stalin as its general secretary. As Rees notes in his chapter, in the early 1930s, the Politburo met regularly, then less frequently as Stalin consolidated all power in his hands. Yet in spite of his growing power, Stalin nevertheless continued throughout this period to involve his "team" in decision making. The Politburo was the "leading organ" of Soviet society, not subordinated to any other institution.

Before the opening of the archives, our stereotype of Soviet planning was that Soviet plans began with the Politburo's assignment of a few basic economic targets, which were then translated by Gosplan into a much larger number of concrete economic targets. We were never sure which targets were set by the dictator and which by Gosplan; nor did we know how they worked together or whether the dictator's planners' preferences were faithfully executed by Gosplan and the industrial ministries. We do know that individual enterprises were not particularly faithful executors of planners' preferences.

Lenin had argued during the early years of Bolshevik rule that the economy could be controlled through its "commanding heights"—heavy industry, transportation, and banking. This principle meant that the dictator need not control *all* aspects of economic life, only the most important. The archives show that, in any case, the Party leadership, with its extremely small staff, could control only a few aspects of economic life. In January 1930, the entire staff of the Central Committee of the Communist Party amounted to only 375 persons, the two largest departments being the secret department (103 persons) and the chancellery department (123). Other departments such as the organizational and instructional department, and the department of culture, employed fewer than 50 persons each.[3] The central Party apparatus had less than 250 persons to assist with the formulation, transmission, and monitoring of planners' preferences. Staffing was also limited in central Soviet (state) institutions; there was a "small Gosplan" within the Council of Ministers, whose branch staffs were spread very thin. For example, all automobile and aviation business was handled by one person and a secretary. The largest central state agency, Gosplan, which at the time included the Central Statistical Administration, employed only 900. Gosplan's department of energy and electrification (one of its most important departments in this period) was staffed by only 30 persons. A Gosplan department head (chemicals section) complained that "we cannot present and decide even one issue because of the complete lack of workers."[4] The major industrial ministries were more generously staffed, with more than 10,000 employees each.

The Party's lack of expert staff meant that most of the actual work of planning and running the Soviet economy had to be carried out by the better-staffed committees such as Gosplan and by the industrial ministries themselves. Clearly, the Politburo could have created a large support staff for itself, but the notion of small staffs was consistent with the Leninist view of the Party as an elite organization. Perhaps those at the top did not want large staffs that might temper their power to decide the key issues of society; they may have felt there were too few "reliable" staffers who could be trusted.

The Politburo did not make all its decisions as a unified body.

3. *Stalinskoe Politbyuro v 30-e Gody* (SP30), ed. O. V. Khlevniuk, A. V. Kvashonkin, L. P. Koshelova, and L. A. Rogovaia (Moscow: AIRO-XX, 1995), pp. 14–15.

4. For examples of the serious complaints from Gosplan departments concerning the lack of personnel, see memos preserved in the Russian State Archive for the Economy (RGAE) from Vagransky (energy and electrification) and Blinov (chemical section) to Gosplan director Kuibyshev. RGAE, f. 4372, op. 39, d. 34, l. 85, and RGAE, f. 4372, op. 39, d. 34, ll. 91–93.

It delegated some decisions to the various Politburo departments, to specific agencies, or to designated individuals, authorizing them to make the decision in the name of the Party: In 1934, the commission on gold reserves was empowered by Stalin to "take all measures in the name of the Politburo which it considers necessary to increase the gold reserves of the USSR." In another decree, dated May 26, 1934, Stalin and two other members were authorized to determine the agenda of a comintern meeting "in the name of the Politburo."[5] By the late 1930s, the most crucial decisions were being taken not by the Politburo but by ad hoc commissions of Politburo members, consisting of five to six members.

The dividing line between the Politburo's "leading role" and Gosplan's "technical" planning role was not absolute. Stalin, in particular, worried about the undue influence of unreliable specialists in Gosplan, even after his massive purge of Gosplan in 1930. In a letter to Molotov, Stalin complained that the Politburo was losing control of important economic decisions to Gosplan, and even worse, to middle-level experts, and he ordered Molotov to "smash the nest of . . . bourgeois politicians in Gosplan, central statistical administration, and so on. Hound them out of Moscow"; "You will see that our funds are being allocated by [Gosplan specialists], while the Politburo is changing from a directing body into a court of appeals, into something like a 'council of elders'."[6] Stalin's concern that specialists must be "loyal" agents meant that key positions must be increasingly occupied by reliable persons. It comes as no surprise that most Poltiburo decisions in the 1930s related to personnel matters.

The Politburo was thus torn between its role of setting the general party line and involvement in detailed decisions. Politburo actions vacillated between general instructions and detailed interventions, and its decisions ranged from trivial matters, such as which factory will get three cars, or who will be allowed to make

5. SP30, p. 16.
6. Lars T. Lih, Oleg V. Naumov, and Oleg V. Khlevniuk, eds., *Stalin's Letters to Molotov, 1925–36* (New Haven, Conn.: Yale University Press, 1995), Letter 44.

a trip abroad, to the setting of the economy's most basic priorities and the approval of its national economic plans. In some cases, the Politburo engaged in protracted discussions of production details, such as whether a particular Soviet car should be a Buick or Ford design, or the proper way to process timber.[7] One case study of vehicles shows that the Politburo and Gosplan had fundamentally different approaches toward resource allocation.[8] Gosplan, charged with producing balances of resources, preferred gradual and balanced changes in allocations; the Politburo valued its ability to "mobilize resources" on short notice. Differences between the Gosplan and Politburo approaches were most evident during periods of supply shocks, when the Politburo radically reshuffled resources contrary to Gosplan's plans for more equal cuts.

THE POLITBURO'S CONTROL FIGURES

Given its limited staffing and need to control the commanding heights, what indicators did the Politburo routinely set that Gosplan used as a basis for national economic plans? The archives show that the Politburo routinely set a rather narrow range of control figures, usually consisting of a relatively small number of physical output targets for key industrial and agricultural commodities. Table 1 shows the Politburo's 1951 *direktivy* control figure targets for the end year of the fifth five-year plan (1955) for national income, investment, consumption, transportation, trade, wages, productivity, and cost reductions. It shows both the figures proposed by Deputy Premier Malenkov and Stalin's corrections in the margin.[9] These Politburo control figures provide growth factors for industrial production, broken down by heavy and light industry, as well as growth factors for various agricultural products.

7. SP30, no. 133, letter from Kaganovich to Ordzhonikidze.
8. Valery Lazarev and Paul Gregory, "Dictators and Cars," Working Papers in International Studies, I-99-6, Hoover Institution, October 1999.
9. These figures are from the XIX Party Congress fond of the Hoover Institution archives (RGASPI, f. 592).

TABLE 1
TARGETS FOR THE FIFTH FIVE-YEAR PLAN

| | GROWTH FACTOR, IN PERCENTS | |
Category	*Politburo/Malenkov proposals, 1951*	*Stalin (margin corrections), 1951*
National income	70%	
Investment	105	
Consumption	50	
Freight turnover	44	
Trade turnover	74	
Costs in industry	− 20	
Industrial labor productivity	52	
Construction labor productivity	47	
Wage fund	30	
Industrial output	80	70%
Group A (intermediate goods)	90	80
Group B (consumer goods)	70	65
Agricultural output		
Grain	35–40	40–50
Wheat	n.a.	55–65
Cotton	55–65	
Flax	35–40	40–50
Sugar beets	60–65	65–70
Sunflower seeds	40–45	50–60
Feed grains	2.5–3	2–3

SOURCE: Hoover archives 2.2590; 592-1-6. 6,37.

The archives show that the most Politburo debate on economic plans was devoted to the size and distribution of the investment budget, denominated in rubles. This is contrary to our long-held assumption that the Soviet economy was planned in physical units, not in value units.[10] The Politburo realized that the investment budget, which itself depended on sales taxes from the population, determined the volume of rubles chasing investment goods.

10. See, e.g., Paul Gregory and Robert Stuart, *Russian and Soviet Economic Structure and Performance* (7th ed., Boston: Addison-Wesley, 2001), chap. 6.

If that budget were too generous, the prices of investment goods—bricks, cement, lumber, machinery—would be bid up. Moreover, the Politburo was conscious of the fact that investment was limited by the size of the state budget insofar as most investment was budget financed. The following account of Stalin's actions at a December 25, 1947, Politburo meeting illustrates these two points:

> Comrade Stalin, upon hearing the deputy ministers of the Council of Ministers, said: The plan is very swollen and is not within our capacity. We should give money only to construction projects that can be placed on line and not spread it out among many projects. They are building all kinds of nonsense in new, unpopulated areas and they are spending a lot of money. It is necessary to expand old factories. Our dear projectors project only new factories and swell construction. It is necessary to set the [investment] plan at 40 billion rubles instead of the mentioned 60 billion. We have to keep in mind that because of the lowering of [consumer] prices and the replacement of the rationing system we have lost 50 billion rubles [from the budget]. If we swell construction, then extra money will appear on the market and there will be devaluation [rise in prices].[11]

The investment budgets in different versions of the fifth five-year plan drawn up between June 1950 and October 1952 illustrate the Politburo's thinking concerning the trade-off between higher investment budgets and higher constructions costs: Table 2 compares the initial investment plan (a 90 percent increase in ruble terms) with the final investment plan (a 60 percent increase), and we see the Poliburo's association of higher investment with higher prices (and the negative association between labor productivity and costs of production). In effect, the smaller investment budget would yield the same amount of "real" investment because of lower costs of production.

The archives reveal that most Politburo discussions of control

---

11. These notes were made by a senior economic official, Malyshev, and are cited in Oleg Khlevnyuk, "Sovetskaia ekonomicheskaia politika na rubezhe 40–50 godov i delo gosplana," Working Paper, Florence, Italy, March 2000.

TABLE 2
DIFFERENT DRAFTS OF THE FIFTH FIVE-YEAR PLAN
(1955 TARGETS, IN PERCENTS)

Category	DATE OF DRAFT				
	June 1950	Jan. 1951	June 1951	Aug. 1951	Oct. 1951
Investment	1.9	2.05	2.13	1.94	1.6
Cost of production	0.85	0.8	0.77	0.79	0.75
Productivity of construction labor	1.45	1.47	1.57	1.55	1.55

figures usually concerned relatively small differences. Some differences, however, could be quite large, such as the remarkable
change in Politburo preferences in 1932, when the Politburo
backed away from the exaggerated planning of the first five-year
plan to adopt more realistic planning for the second five-year
plan. In July of 1932, the Politburo ordered a special commission
to consider reducing the investment budget. The commission,
headed by the chairman of Gosplan, proposed reducing planned
investment by 10 percent "with the aim of bringing the amount
of finance provided into conformity with the physical volume of
work indicated in the plan and concentrating material resources
on the crucial [construction] sites,"[12] as well as correcting the previous policy of spreading investment over a large number of projects to avoid the piling-up of incomplete construction projects.
Stalin agreed with a marginal note: "Is this necessary [the excessive spreading of investment]? It is not necessary!"[13] In spite of
protests from industrial ministers whose investment budgets were
being cut (including protests from the influential minister of heavy
industry and Stalin confidant, G. K. Ordzhonikidze), the Politburo remained firm. Molotov silenced protests by declaring that

12. R. W. Davies, *Crisis and Progress in the Soviet Economy, 1931–33* (London: Macmillan, 1996), p. 230.
13. R. W. Davies and O. Khlevnyuk, "Gosplan," in E. A. Rees, ed., *Decision-
making in the Stalinist Command Economy* (London: Macmillan, 1997), p. 41.

Stalin himself supported the cuts. In 1933, there were further efforts to restrain investment, supported by the Ministry of Finance's claim that a budget surplus was necessary to reduce inflationary pressures.

The story behind the Politburo's 1932 move toward moderation tells much about its relationship with its planner, Gosplan. In July of 1931, Gosplan, which was headed by a key Politburo member and Stalin deputy, proposed to move away from the overambitious plans of the first five-year plan period. Gosplan had been purged just a year earlier for supporting moderate plans and would not have taken this step without approval from Stalin, who, after consultation, agreed to a significant lowering of pig-iron targets. Another player in this episode was Ordzhonikidze, whose engineering reports showed that the ambitious metallurgy target for 1937 (45 million tons of pig iron) could not be met. The minister explained that his own iron plants produced only 5 million tons in 1930. In August of 1931, Gosplan proposed to reduce the 1937 pig-iron target to 25–30 million tons. In November of 1931, the Politburo approved a further significant reduction in pig-iron production, from 17 to 9–10 million tons for 1932.[14]

From the early 1930s to his death in 1953, Stalin was the Politburo's ultimate decision maker. Stalin's letter to Molotov of September 12, 1933, is indicative of his role: "Greetings Viacheslav [Molotov]: (1) I agree that we should not go higher than 21 billion rubles for capital work for 1934 and that the growth of industrial production—not more than 15 percent. (2) I also am agreed that gross grain collections for 1932 must be 698 million centners—not less."[15] Another letter from the minister of transportation and Politburo member to the minister of heavy industry (and Politburo member) of September 4, 1935, gives a flavor for

14. Oleg Khlevnyuk, "The People's Commissariat of Heavy Industry," in ibid., p. 105.

15. Letter from Stalin to Molotov of September 12, 1933, cited in SP30, p. 133.

Politburo actions: "Today we [the Politburo] just decided, on the basis of Stalin's proposal, to buy, in addition to our collections, 300 million puds of grain. . . . Today we discussed the 4th quarter plan and they added 100 million rubles to your annual limit."[16] These proposals had been sent to Sochi, where Stalin was vacationing, for his approval. It was customary for Politburo decisions to be forwarded to Stalin if he were away. Often Prime Minister Molotov would inform Stalin of the decision; in a number of cases, Stalin refused to approve Politburo or Council of Ministers decisions, thereby effectively killing them.

Stalin was not, however, above listening to his close associates and being persuaded to change his mind. According to a document of the Council of Ministers—probably immediately after a meeting of the Politburo on December 25, 1947—Stalin, in spite of his earlier decision to limit capital investment in 1947 to 40 billion rubles, was persuaded by the chairman of Gosplan and Deputy Prime Minister Voznesensky to raise the capital limit to 50 billion. This revised figure was confirmed the next day by the Politburo. The final figure signed by Stalin raised capital investment to 55 billion. Thanks to Voznesensky's interventions, Stalin's original proposal was raised to from 40 to 55 billion—almost one third.[17]

Why was someone like Voznesensky able to change Stalin's mind? Unlike many of his Politburo associates, Voznesensky held strong personal opinions. Consider Stalin's praise of Voznesensky:

Unlike other associates who mask disagreements by either agreeing or pretending to agree among themselves before coming to me, Voznesensky, if he is not in agreement, does not agree on paper. He comes to me and expresses his disagreement. They understand that I can't know everything and they want to make me a rubber stamp. I pay attention to disagreements, to disputes, why they arose, what

16. SP30, no. 130.
17. Khlevnyuk, Working Paper, 2000.

is going on. But they try to hide them from me. They vote and then they hide. . . . That is why I prefer the objections of Voznesensky to their agreements.[18]

It should be noted that Voznesensky paid with his life for his independence. His Politburo colleagues conspired against him, resulting in his eventual execution for treason.[19]

BARGAINING

Were the dictator's preferences set exogenously in stone or were they influenced by the bargaining of those who had to fulfill them? The archives reveal intense bargaining over control figures, focused on two central issues: reductions in output targets and increases in investment. Even during the period of exaggerated expectations prior to 1932, Stalin and the Politburo were not impervious to appeals for realism. As Rees notes in his chapter, Stalin was persuaded by regional party officials that their regions could not meet their grain delivery quotas during the impending famine of 1932–33 and agreed to lower their collection targets and allot them more seed.

Bargaining was inevitable in such a system: For the most part, the highest production officials—the industrial and transportation ministers—were Politburo members, which meant that they had the political clout to fight for resources within the Politburo. Once appointed to industrial positions, the Politburo member viewed himself in a struggle against those who represented the "national interest," such as Gosplan. A quote on these natural conflicts appears in the memoirs of a Politburo member and Stalin deputy (Kaganovich) concerning the change that occurred after being appointed Minister of Transportation:

When we [Kaganovich and Molotov] worked together in the Central Committee, we worked in a friendly manner, but when he became

18. Quoted in ibid.
19. Ibid., p. 13.

Prime Minister and I Minister of Transportation we argued on business matters. I demanded more rails, more capital investment, and [Gosplan] did not give and Molotov supported Gosplan. I was on the same footing with Ordzhonkidze [Minister of Heavy Industry]—he also argued and fought with Molotov about capital investment, about relations with industry. And we complained to Stalin. And Molotov wanted us to complain to the Council of Ministers. But we considered that the Politburo was the highest decision-making body.[20]

When disputes arose between producers and central organizations, "compromise" commissions were often formed to find solutions that suited both sides. In fact, the most powerful ministries often rejected the compromises offered by such commissions and chose to fight out their dispute, using delays and threats of lost production.[21] In other cases, the parties accepted the compromise. Consider the protest of the Gorky region against an "unrealistic" timber production target. Gosplan had assigned a target of 25 million mcm, which local trusts and local party officials had requested to lower to 23 million mcm. On November 3, 1935, a meeting of the Ad Hoc Commission on the Question of Procurement of Timber in Gorky Region was called, attended by local Gorky representatives, the chairman of Gosplan, the Minister of Timber Industry, the Commissioner of Fuel, and Gosplan's timber sector chief. The special commission refused Gorky officials' request to lower the production target but ordered the allotment to the region of fifty additional tractors. This bargaining outcome was typical: Requests to lower output targets were denied but producers were given the wherewithal to meet the production target. On October 1, 1935, Gosplan countered the Ministry of Heavy Industry's production plan, which had asked for a production growth of 19.7 percent and growth of labor productivity of 13.5 percent, with a production increase of 28–30 percent and a

20. F. Chuev, *Tak govoril Kaganovich* (Moscow, 1993), p. 61.
21. Eugenia Belova and Paul Gregory, "Dictators, Loyal and Opportunistic Agents, and Punishment," unpublished paper, Florence, Italy, July 2000.

labor productivity increase of 25–26 percent, and called for cost reductions of no less than 9 percent.[22] The ministry agreed to a 26 percent increase in output, labor productivity growth of 20 percent, and cost reductions of 6 percent but demanded an increase in capital investment of 1.5 billion. As the ministry's response shows, the difference between the two sets of figures was rather small. The final figures accepted by the Politburo gave the ministry one half of its requested investment increase.

The archives also provide ample evidence that bargaining power depended on political influence. Ordzhonikidze, as a close associate of Stalin and a member of the Politburo, commanded considerable bargaining power for the Ministry of Heavy Industry. The Ministry of Transportation was starved of investment resources until Kaganovich, also a close Stalin associate and Politburo member, was appointed minister of transportation in February 1935; after Kaganovich's appointment, external supervision over the Ministry of Transportation, which had been such an irritation to the previous minister, virtually ceased. Within a year, Kaganovich had succeeded in raising investment resources for transportation despite the opposition of Gosplan.[23]

PRIORITIES AND INTERVENTIONS

The commanding-heights philosophy argued that the economy could be controlled by controlling a few key commodities. This chapter has shown that the Politburo set control figures for a few basic targets in physical terms along with investment targets in rubles and cost, price, and productivity targets. As the chapter by Tikhonov and Gregory shows, even the more generously staffed Gosplan could set targets in the early postwar period for only 127 products and provide 66 agency breakdowns for investment. Once approved, these control figures were subject to considerable

22. Khlevnyuk, "People's Commissariat," p. 121.
23. E. A. Rees, "The People's Commissariat of Transport (Railways)," in Rees, ed., *Decision-Making*, pp. 203–34.

manipulation and distortion by the industrial ministries and their enterprises. The Politburo's ability to control the economy through its control of the investment budget and a few physical control figures was extremely limited. Because it could not control investment costs, it was unable to control the allocation of physical investment. Moreover, the industrial ministries fought against specific targets and against specificity in its investment plan to gain as much freedom from central control as possible. The ministries typically resisted presenting figures broken down by enterprises, and they did not even tell central authorities what investment projects would cost—though Gosplan did all it could to wring this information out of them. They presented information as late as possible and in as little detail as possible, often setting off intense battles with Gosplan as the Politburo's prime representative.

The Politburo had other means of controlling the basic direction of the economy. It set priorities, made direct ad hoc interventions in the allocation of resources, and maintained direct control over some key commodities. Politburo priorities could be either general or quite specific. In the former category, consider this priority statement issued by the Politburo in September 1932 concerning the distribution of vehicles to organizations: "Preserve the position of current users with a slight growth of supply to light industry firms producing items of mass consumption, continue the policy of mechanization of agriculture, and give preference to union over regional organizations."[24] Stalin's priorities issued in July 1935 were more specific: "There are some things that must not be reduced: NKO, locomotives under the ministry of transportation allocation, the building of schools—under the ministry of education; re-equipment under light industry; paper and cellulose factories—under the heading 'Timber;' some very necessary enterprises (enumerated) under the [ministry of heavy industry]. This makes it more difficult. We shall see."[25]

24. September Plenum of the Politburo, 1932.
25. Davies and Khlevnyuk, "Gosplan," p. 55.

Planners' preferences were also set via the numerous interventions into resource allocation decisions made by the Politburo and its state executive arm, Sovnarkom. The early Soviet theorists of planning had never intended planning to be perfect. Although they expected aggregate planning to be accurate, they anticipated that numerous corrections would have to be made by political authorities to correct micro planning defects. The archives reveal that interventions represented perhaps the most burdensome task of the Politburo as it responded to thousands of requests and petitions for plan alterations or resource increases. An example of this is vehicle planning. Although the first-quarter 1933 vehicle distribution plan had already been approved, the Politburo made two significant interventions: first, the Kazak Regional (Party) Committee, after pointing out its shortage of transport for emergency grain supplies, was the beneficiary of a special Politburo decree that increased its truck allocation by a factor of three;[26] second, the Politburo ordered a radical change in car distribution, allocating 90 percent to "organs of control over agricultural producers."[27] These are only two examples of Politburo interventions into one single quarterly plan that effectively rendered the original plan inoperable. Another means of enforcing planners' preferences was for the dictator to allocate resources directly. This was done by a number of ad hoc commissions headed by prominent Politburo members, such as the foreign exchange commission, or the Molotov commission that allocated vehicles. A case study of vehicles shows how this was done.[28]

COMMUNICATION AND ENFORCEMENT

Stalin worried openly that the Politburo could issue decrees that would either not be communicated to the proper parties or,

---

26. State Archive of the Russian Federation (GARF), f. 5446, op. 14a, d. 628, ll. 143–44; Russian State Archive of Contemporary History (RGASPI), f. 17, op. 3, d. 914, ll. 10–11.

27. RGASPI, f. 17, op. 3, d. 915, l. 8.

28. Lazarev and Gregory, "Dictators and Cars."

worse, would be ignored. In his letters to Molotov, Stalin expressed a number of concerns: In a letter of September 22, 1930, he proposed to establish, "under the Council of Commissars, a standing commission [Commission on Fulfillment] for the sole purpose of systematically checking on the fulfillment of the center's decisions. . . . Without such reforms the center's directives will remain completely on paper." In an earlier letter, dated August 21, 1929, he confided to Molotov: "The Politburo has adopted my proposal concerning grain procurement. This is good, but in my opinion, it is inadequate. Now the problem is *fulfilling* the Politburo's decision. There is no need to insist that all procurement agencies (especially in Ukraine) will evade this decision. Furthermore, I am afraid that the local GPU will not learn about the Politburo's decision, and it [the decision] will get bogged down in the bowels of the OGPU." In a letter of August-September 1930, Stalin wrote Molotov: "I think it would be beneficial if the Central Committee plenums were to move away from general decrees on general issues and hear reports—real reports—from the economic commissariats that are doing badly."[29] For these reasons, an extensive system of control was established, which is described in the chapters by Rees and Belova.

Politburo decrees were formulated either in the name of the Party or according to "Soviet order" as directives of the Council of Ministers. All were signed by the prime minister (Molotov) or by one of his deputies. The most important decisions were issued as joint decrees of the Central Committee of the Communist Party and the Council of Ministers. Party decrees were never broadly circulated, but were sent to Party committees as statements of intent. A short explanation signed by Molotov accompanied all draft decrees, justifying the proposed action. Copies of these documents were filed in the secret department of affairs management of Sovnarkom, which was responsible for correspondence with the Politburo. After confirmation by the Politburo, a notation was

29. Lih, Naumov, and Khlevniuk, *Stalin's Letters*, Letters 42, 61, and 68.

made on the copy of the number and date of the decision. The
originals were filed as materials to the protocols of the Politburo.[30] The secret department circulated Politburo decrees to a
specified list of officials according to special instructions. Politburo decrees were classified as either "absolutely secret" (*sovers-
henno sekretno*) or, in the most confidential cases, they were
placed in a "special file" (*osobaia papka*). The communication
system of the Ministry of Interior's police was regularly used to
distribute these documents. According to budget documents of
the Politburo, between January and September of 1932, between
1,500 and 6,100 documents were dispatched monthly through the
secret police at a cost of 31,000 rubles for the period.[31]

Although a rigid system of distribution existed on paper, Politburo document distribution was plagued by lax discipline. Secret
documents were supposed to be returned by recipients within a
specified period of time, but a 1933 survey showed that only 40
percent were actually returned; for example, the deputy minister
of heavy industry had received eighteen copies but had returned
only five.[32] The Politburo imposed sanctions on the most negligent
recipients, such as withdrawing the right to receive further documents.[33]

Given the lack of staff of Soviet and party central organizations, the interpretation of the general party line had to be left to
a number of subordinate organizations. Execution of central orders was monitored and enforced in an overlapping fashion by
the Soviet (state) and party apparatus and by various independent
enforcement agencies, such as military inspectors and the secret
police. Each local, regional, and republican party office (*obkom,
kraikom*, republic central committees) was ordered "to place the
responsibility on one of its secretaries for monitoring the fulfill-

30. SP30, p. 17.
31. SP30, no. 12.
32. SP30, nos. 75, 76.
33. A Central Asian party official (Ikraimova), for example, was punished for
leaving protocols in his room in the Hotel National and was deprived of the right to
receive documents for three months (SP30, no. 75).

ment of directives of the Central Committee of the Communist Party and the responsibility for timely responses to related questions." Similarly, ministries were ordered to designate one member of the collegium to be responsible for monitoring fulfillment of party directives, following more detailed instructions on deadlines and reporting than those imposed on party organizations. In keeping with the general policy of secrecy, "persons having the right to be informed about decisions of the Central Committee are categorically forbidden to reveal, when these decisions are passed through their structures, that these are instructions of the Central Committee."[34]

OUT-OF-CONTROL LOCAL OFFICIALS

Local party organizations proved to be a problem for the Politburo in the early 1930s. Their out-of-control excesses during the 1929–30 purges of industrial managers and experts (the so-called Shakhty Affair) illustrate the danger of allowing "loyal" local party officials to interpret the party line. Stalin, in 1929, unleashed a campaign against "wrecker" experts and managers. The campaign against wreckers and saboteurs was carried out largely by local party, militia, and state organizations, with the assistance of the secret policy (the OGPU). Many managers and specialists were imprisoned, directors were fired, local party officials took over management, and some executions took place. Managers from the Donbass region reported that over half of their specialists were in prison. After the disastrous effects on production of the campaign against wreckers became apparent in 1930, the Politburo took steps to stop the campaign. The new minister of Heavy Industry (Ordzhonikidze), an early supporter of the purge, delivered at a conference of January–February, 1931, attended by Stalin, a strong report strengthening management and stating that the mass of workers had nothing to do with the wreckers.[35] This

34. SP30, nos. 83, 84, 85.
35. Khlevnyuk, Working Paper, p. 97.

retreat was supported by Stalin (the archives contain Stalin's marginal notes on Ordzhonikidze's draft). The Politburo adopted Stalin's instruction on January 20, 1931, to local party organizations not "to allow the removal of directors of works of all-union significance without the sanction of the Central Committee and of the Supreme Economic Council."

Ignoring clear-cut Politburo instructions, local party organizations, local militia, and OGPU officials continued their harassment of managers and specialists. In February of 1931, Ordzhonikidze received a letter from a Rostov director that the regional party organization had dismissed the factory committee and had placed its managers in the factory and turned managers and specialists over to the OGPU and courts. On March 17, the Rostov party organization was censured for breaching Politburo directives. In August, the Central Committee again had to dismiss a local party leader for substituting local party leaders for local managers. In May and June of 1931, the Politburo had to assure an accused plant director of "normal working conditions of work in the shop . . . and that the North Caucusus regional party committee would end the practice of interrogating specialists by the militia." Party organizations were not allowed to revoke, correct, or delay operative orders issued by the factory management. On June 22–23, 1931, the Central Committee convened a special meeting to address the harassment of management.

After the June meeting, the government adopted additional laws to protect managers and specialists, affirming that no director could be arrested without the agreement of the corresponding ministry. Disputes were to be referred to the Central Committee. But local party organizations still proved difficult to restrain: The Central Committee had to issue rebukes against local party interference as late as April of 1933, more than two years after the Politburo had called off the campaign against wreckers.

The Politburo's negative experience with local party organizations prompted it to centralize punitive powers in the Ministry of Interior and in the Procurator's office, the two offices that provided the venue for the Great Terror of the late 1930s.[36] Additionally, in 1934, as is explained in the chapters by Rees and Belova, the work of party and state control commissions was centralized and a structure was established that was supposedly independent of local organizations.

By the mid 1930s, the Politburo faced growing awareness of an additional danger of relying on local party organizations to interpret and execute planners' preferences: Local party organizations were not "honest brokers"; rather they lobbied for the interests of enterprises in their region. As noted above, timber trusts in the Gorky region felt that their 1935 production target was unrealistic. Instead of protesting to their own ministry, they solicited the support of local state and party organizations, who sent a telegram to Gosplan requesting a plan reduction, citing technical problems, distance from rivers, difficulty of floating logs down the river, and lack of horses. The meeting of the special commission formed to resolve this dispute was attended by local party officials.[37] The point of this example is that local party authorities were acting in the interests of local enterprises to alter a production target that had been approved by Gosplan, the timber ministry, and the Council of Ministers.

CONCLUSIONS

Planners' preferences is a misnomer. The system's preferences were formed not by the planners in Gosplan but by the political leadership in the party's Politburo. The system's preferences were not expressed only in plans; they were expressed in priorities and, perhaps most important in the 1930s, by direct interventions. We can posit two different models of the manner in which the Soviet dictator formed planners' preferences. The hierarchical model starts with the Politburo and Stalin, with distinct preferences, a

36. Khlevnyuk, "People's Commissariat," pp. 101–3.
37. On this, see Rees, "The People's Commissariat of the Timber Industry," Rees, ed., *Decision-Making*, pp. 133–34.

well-defined party line and a well-organized planning and control apparatus, which then tries to get the preferences implemented down the line to the individual enterprise.[38] The bargaining model starts with agents at each level of the planning hierarchy, having their own preferences, who bargain for scarce resources. The bargaining goes up to the Politburo, but is decided there not according to a well-defined party line but according to the power position of the agents. Were the economic directives of the Politburo the result of "bottom up" planning, whereby the industrial ministries proposed production plans and bargained for resources, or of "top down" planning, in which the Politburo simply dictated to the industrial ministries what they were to produce and allotted them supplies of resources?

What have we learned from the Soviet state and party archives on these matters? First, the Soviet state and party archives clearly show that, in spite of the growing Stalin dictatorship, the bargaining model was in widespread use. When economic agents protested plans, there was usually some accommodation or compromise offered. The bargaining model appears to be unavoidable in such a system, in which some of the most important leaders are held responsible for concrete results. It is noteworthy that, with a few exceptions, bargaining was over relatively small differences.

Second, the Soviet dictator did not rely exclusively on its power to set basic control figures for the economy that Gosplan would translate into concrete plans. The dictator controlled too few targets, had too small a staff, and knew of the vast potential for abuse by production organization, ranging from the large ministries headed by fellow Politburo members down to individual enterprises. The dictator tried to expand its power over resource allocation by setting priorities, which it hoped participants would follow, but this proved to be a weak form of control. The most potent means of control appeared to be interventions directly in

38. I am indebted to Hans-Juergen Wagener for this classification.

the process of resource allocation. These ad hoc interventions were disruptive to the normal planning process, but the dictator felt they were necessary, because even its most trusted agents in Gosplan were "specialists," whose loyalty and judgment were not secure.

Third, throughout the 1930s, the dictator had a great deal of difficulty in dividing turf between itself and Gosplan; the line between policy and operations was difficult to draw, and much of the dictator's resources were dissipated in solving relatively trivial resource-allocation issues.

Fourth, the dictator learned that only the center would look after the center's interests. The industrial ministries and territorial authorities were concerned about achieving "good" results in their backyards. Even local party, secret police, and militia, which theoretically should follow the party line, were untrustworthy. The dictator's apparent inability to control local officials may require historians to rethink Stalin's blame of local officials for excesses during forced collectivization in his famous "Dizzy from Success" article in *Pravda*. Ministries hid information from the center, refused to present disaggregated targets, abused any decentralized authority offered them, and sought as much independence of action as possible. Hence, as time passed, the dictator attempted to centralize the control function—the process of monitoring the execution of the dictator's orders. Although there existed a highly formalized systems of checks and balances on the execution of the dictator's orders, it is unlikely that even formally assigned controllers would set aside their own vested interests to represent the "true" interests of the party.

3

LEADERS AND THEIR INSTITUTIONS

E. A. Rees

The Stalinist regime was one of the most tyrannical regimes in human history. It is therefore not surprising that scholars should be interested in knowing more about the genesis of such a system, about Stalin as a personality, and about the nature of the regime: how it was organised, how it worked; what measure of influence was exerted by other leaders apart from Stalin, and what influence institutional lobbies or social pressures had in shaping this regime. These question have a wider significance, because the nature of the political regime had a direct bearing on the way in which policy was formulated, and on the way in which the system evolved over time (on these matters see the chapter by Davies).

KNOWLEDGE PRIOR TO THE OPENING OF THE ARCHIVES

Before the party and governmental archives began to be opened from the early 1990s onward our knowledge on the workings of the Soviet system was patchy. We relied on a limited number of sources: official pronouncements, laws and resolutions passed by leading party and government bodies, the speeches and statements by leading figures, press and journal articles, and accounts by émigrés. Our knowledge of the 1920s, when debate was more open, was greater than for the 1930s and the 1940s. We studied the party-state apparatus to explain the way in which the political system had changed from the 1920s; the impact of the defeat of the Left and Right opposition, the drive toward greater internal party discipline, the closure of debate, and the rise of Stalin to supreme power.

Prior to the opening of the archives historians of all tendencies recognized the profound changes in the Soviet political system that were associated with the rise of Stalin. Within the party there was the decline in the influence of the party congress and the Central Committee, and the concentration of power within the central party bodies—the Politburo, Orgburo, and Secretariat. With this went a decline of the party itself: the end of internal party democracy, the institution of regular purges of the party ranks, the transition of the party from a forum of policy debate into an instrument for managing the economy, and the shift from the recruitment of proletarians into the party to a recruitment policy that, after 1939, favored those with higher education.

Alongside the changes in the party went major changes in the state apparatus: first, the growing importance of the economic administrative apparatus, reflected in the proliferation of economic commissariats; second, the growing role of the NKVD, associated with collectivization, "dekulakization," the administration of the burgeoning labor camp system, and the growing suppression of internal dissent; third, the growing role of the military, associated with the threat posed by Japan in the Far East, and by Germany under Hitler from 1933 onward.

All this was generally accepted. The developments in the 1930s were seen by most scholars as confirming the transition to a "totalitarian" regime, exhibiting the six points elaborated by Friedrich and Brzezinski, who viewed the political system as a pyramidal structure, within which conflict between institutions was consciously devised to maximize the leaders' personal power, in which the flow of influence was overwhelmingly top-down, and in which the society was reduced to an inert, atomized mass.[1] An alternative perspective was offered by Trotsky, who sought to analyze developments from a Marxist perspective, depicting Stalinism as a form of Soviet Bonapartism, which was characterized by the rise in the power of the bureaucracy.[2]

Khrushchev's secret speech in 1956 and his subsequent memoirs added flesh to the bones.[3] From 1934 onward, Khrushchev argued, the system of collective leadership within the Politburo broke down, allowing the establishment of Stalin's personal dictatorship, euphemistically referred to as the "cult of personality." Thereafter major policies emanated from Stalin—the purges were largely his creation; the blunders of June 1941 and the early phase of the war were his responsibility; errors in the period of postwar construction were his.

Various sources sought to fill in the details concerning the internal workings of the Soviet political system in this period. One account, which appears to originate with Boris Nicolaevsky, asserted that from 1930 onward the Politburo was split between two factions—liberal and hard-line.[4] At crucial stages Stalin's power was checked by the Politburo. His demand for the execution of M. N. Ryutin in 1932, it was asserted, was blocked by the Politburo. In these struggles Stalin tended to occupy the middle ground, until the deaths of Gosplan chairman V. V. Kuibyshev in 1934 and Commissar of Heavy Industry G. K. Ordzhonikidze in 1937, when the balance shifted to the hard-liners whom Stalin then backed. Another account, again originating with Nicolaevsky, argued that at the XVII Party Congress a disgruntled faction in the party sought to canvass opinion on removing Stalin from

1. Carl J. Friedrich and Zbigniew K. Brzezinski, *Totalitarian Dictatorship and Autocracy* (New York: Praeger, 1956).

2. L. Trotsky, *The Revolution Betrayed* (London: New Park, 1967; first published 1937).

3. N. S. Khrushchev, *The Secret Speech*, ed. Zh. Medvedev and R. Medvedev (Nottingham: Spokesman Books, 1976).

4. Boris Nicolaevsky, *Power and the Soviet Elite* (London, 1960).

the post of General Secretary and replacing him with the supposedly more moderate S. M. Kirov, party chief of Leningrad. This
was the reason for the murder of Kirov (at which Khrushchev
hinted at the XX Party Congress in 1956) and the subsequent
annihilation of most of the Central Committee elected in 1934
and a large proportion of the XVII Party Congress delegates.

Exactly how much power Stalin exercised remained unclear.
Some argued that already at the time of Lenin's death in 1924
Stalin was the effective ruler of the country. Others stressed the
celebrations of his fiftieth birthday in December 1929 as marking
the establishment of his personal dictatorship and the growth of
the Stalin "cult." Some saw the terror of 1936–1938 as the period
when he established his unquestioned power.

Prior to the opening of the archives historians sought to piece
together how the central party and government bodies worked in
practice, particularly using accounts emanating from Soviet émigrés. The most comprehensive attempt to analyze these processes
was undertaken by Niels Erik Rosenfeldt in his book *Knowledge
and Power*, which placed great emphasis on the subdepartments
of the Secretariat and Orgburo, and on Stalin's private office, as
the main centers in which policy was formulated and its implementation supervised, and control over cadres regulated. Within
this system a key role was assigned to Stalin's private secretary,
A. N. Pokrebyshev.[5]

In the 1980s as part of the general reappraisal of Soviet history
by a younger generation of historians most of these basic assumptions were called into question. J. Arch Getty in his reinterpreta-
tion of the terror in his 1985 book *The Origins of the Great
Purges* questioned much of the work written on the 1930s, particularly as it related to how central a role Stalin played in events;

5. Niels Erik Rosenfeldt, *Knowledge and Power: The Role of Stalin's Secret
Chancellery in the Soviet System of Government* (Copenhagen, 1978). A more wide-
ranging survey of the Stalinist party-state apparatus (before the opening of the archives) is provided by Graeme J. Gill, *The Origins of the Stalinist Political System*
(Cambridge: Cambridge University Press, 1990).

he argued that the influence of other individuals and even groups within the higher party leadership should be examined. Central to this new "revisionist" approach was the argument that the totalitarian version distorted the true nature of the Soviet regime, which should be viewed much more in terms of a system of bureaucratic politics and social pressures, a system of imperfect controls, in which Stalin and the leaders around him were not fully in control.

The opening of the party and state archives has given scholars access to the stenographic reports of the Central Committee plenums, to the protocols of the Politburo, and even, for some privileged scholars, access to the Politburo's special files (*osobaya papka*). In addition, we have the correspondence between Stalin and his leading deputies V. M. Molotov and L. M. Kaganovich, for the early 1930s.[6] We now also have the appointments diary of those who met Stalin in his Kremlin office throughout the period.[7] Interviews with Stalin's closest deputies add further insights.[8] The availability of the protocols of the Soviet government's Council of People's Commissars (Sovnarkom) has also greatly increased our understanding of the decision-making process.

THE CENTRAL PARTY BODIES: THE POLITBURO

From its formal establishment in 1919 the Politburo was the supreme decision-making body in the ruling Communist Party. It was formally elected by the party Central Committee and was answerable before the party Central Committee and party congress. The Politburo in the 1920s acquired immense power and status, but its work was always shrouded in mystery. After 1922

6. Lars T. Lih, Oleg V. Naumov, and Oleg V. Khlevnyuk, eds., *Stalin's Letters to Molotov 1925–36* (New Haven, Conn.: Yale University Press, 1995); R. W. Davies et al., eds., *The Stalin-Kaganovich Letters* (New Haven, Conn.: Yale University Press, forthcoming).

7. *Istoricheskii arkhiv*, 1994, no. 6; 1995, nos. 2, 3, 4, 5–6; 1997, no. 1; 1998, no. 4.

8. F. Chuev, *Sto sorok besed s Molotovym iz dnevnika F. Chueva* (Moscow, 1991); F. Chuev, *Tak govoril Kaganovich* (Moscow, 1993).

leadership of the Politburo became associated with the post of party General Secretary, Stalin's position in the party. With the progressive fusion of the party and state institutions, the Politburo was recognized as not only the supreme party body but also the ultimate authority to which all other institutions, including the Soviet government, headed by Sovnarkom, were subordinate.

With the opening of the archives Stalin's stature in the 1920s now appears greater than was previously appreciated. Stalin played a decisive role in policy making from the time of Lenin's death onward. Stalin was not, as has commonly been asserted, a poor third, an undistinguished mediocrity after Trotsky and G. E. Zinoviev contending for the succession. He was, in fact, among those in the know, the favorite to succeed Lenin. He was already reputed as a skilled political fighter, a man with a formidable capacity for administrative work, and known for his independent cast of mind and iron will. The defeat of the Left and Right Oppositions consolidated his control over the Politburo, but from 1928 to 1932 the Politburo remained a force, although Stalin was certainly more than *primus inter pares* within the ruling oligarchy. Policy declarations by Stalin were seen as having as much, if not more, authority than a decision by the Politburo collectively.

But Stalin triumphed not only because he was able to bend events to his will but also because of his ability to adapt himself to circumstances. Though Stalinism as a regime was in many ways fundamentally different from Leninism, the knowledge that we now have of the early Bolshevik regime (particularly of the Red Terror of 1918 and of Bolshevik policies of repression) suggest that the interconnection between the two was much stronger than previously understood. The period of the New Economic Policy of the 1920s now appears as a brief interlude between War Communism and the Stalinist "revolution from above," and the possibilities of an alternative third way (whether that espoused by L. D. Trotsky, or that advanced by N. I. Bukharin) appear more tenuous. This revolution set in train profound changes in the organization of the party-state apparatus and in state-societal relations that marked the Soviet regime until its demise in 1991.

Even regular meetings of the Politburo from 1924 to 1930 did not guarantee collective decision making. In the years 1923–1925 Trotsky complained repeatedly that Stalin and his allies resolved key decisions prior to the Politburo's meetings. L. B. Kamenev at the XIV Party Congress in 1926 bitterly denounced the near-dictatorial powers of the General Secretary. In 1928 the Right opposition were outmaneuvered in the Politburo by Stalin's ruse as General Secretary of according casting votes to members of the presidium of the Central Control Commission (TsKK). In the autumn of 1930 S. E. Syrtsov, in an outspoken attack on Stalin, protested at the decline of the Politburo as a collective decision-making body, with certain members being excluded from its deliberations.[9]

The defeat of the Right in 1929 allowed Stalin to consolidate the dominant position of his own faction within the party leadership. The Politburo following the Central Committee plenum of February 4, 1932, consisted of the following members:[10]

MEMBERS

I. V. Stalin	General Secretary
L. M. Kaganovich	party secretary, secretary Moscow party organization
S. M. Kirov	secretary of Leningrad party organization
S. V. Kosior	secretary of Ukrainian party organization
V. M. Molotov	chairman of Sovnarkom
V. V. Kuibyshev	chair of Gosplan
G. K. Ordzhonikidze	commissar of Heavy Industry
A. A. Andreev	commissar of Transportation
K. E. Voroshilov	commissar of Defense
M. Kalinin	chairman of the Central Executive Committee USSR

9. O. V. Khlevynuk et al., eds., *Stalinskoe Politbyuro v 30–3 gody: Sbornik dokumentov* (Moscow, 1995), pp. 94–112.

10. E. A. Rees, ed., *Decision-Making in the Stalinist Command Economy, 1932–37* (London: Macmillan, 1997), pp. 9–10.

CANDIDATES

A. I. Mikoyan	commissar of Supply
V. Ya. Chubar'	chairman of Sovnarkom Ukraine SSR
G. I. Petrovskii	chairman of the Central Executive Committee of Ukraine SSR

The ten full members and three candidate members reflected a particular system of representation at the highest level of the party. The heads of the main party and government institutions were always represented: the General Secretary of the party, the chairman of Sovnarkom, and the chairman of the Central Executive Committee USSR. The most important local party bodies (Moscow, Leningrad, and the Ukraine), and key institutions, like Gosplan, and the commissariats of defense, heavy industry, and rail transport, were also represented. The head of the Central Control Commission (TsKK), which was responsible for enforcing party discipline, was required during his term of office to formally surrender his membership of the Politburo, but he attended its meetings. All members of the Central Committee and of the Presidium of the Central Control Commission were entitled to attend Politburo meetings, but without voting rights. A typical meeting on March 28, 1929, had in attendance eight Politburo members, three Politburo candidate members, twenty-two Central Committee members, eleven Central Committee candidate members, and seven members of the presidium of the Central Control Commission

The Politburo's protocols provide a great deal of information about decision making in the Stalin era. They list those attending, the agenda of the meeting, and the decisions taken, often with the text of the approved resolutions appended. The protocols were signed by Stalin, and after 1930, in his absence, by Kaganovich, the second Secretary. The protocols, however, are not stenographic reports of the Politburo meetings (which apparently do not exist) and from them alone it is impossible to deduce the positions taken by individuals in policy disputes. The protocols provide no information on voting in the Politburo; the working practice was to proceed on the basis of consensus, avoiding the divisive practice of voting on issues. The protocols provide little information on the way business was conducted, although from other sources it appears that the meetings were generally chaired by Molotov.

The Politburo concentrated on six main areas of policy: international affairs, defense, internal security, heavy industry, agriculture, and transport. The protocols are least revealing regarding the first three, which tend to be dealt with in the secret files (*osobaya papka*). The protocols indicate clearly that at least on a formal level the Politburo was supreme. Decrees issued in the name of Sovnarkom or the Central Executive Committee were almost without fail approved beforehand by the Politburo. Politburo decisions might be issued either as Central Committee resolutions, as joint Central Committee–Sovnarkom or government decrees, or even as orders (*prikazy*) of a particular commissariat. The protocols record the Politburo's confirmation of a vast number of nomenklatura appointments, which in most cases had been processed by the party's Orgburo.

The Politburo protocols vividly illustrate how far the system of leadership changed in the decade following Lenin's death. Up until September 1929 collective leadership was based on regular weekly meetings of the Politburo, almost invariably on a Thursday. The main change in the Politburo's power and status came in 1932 and 1933. In 1932 there were forty-seven meetings, but Stalin attended only thirty, being absent from all meetings between June 1 and September 1. In 1933 there were twenty-four meetings, in 1934 only eighteen, in 1935 just fifteen, and in 1936 a mere nine. In the first six months of 1937, six meetings of the Politburo were listed; in the second half of the year none. In 1938 there were four meetings, in 1939 and 1940 just two meetings each.[11]

11. On the meetings of the Politburo, see E. A. Rees, "Stalin, the Politburo and Rail Transport Policy," in Julian Cooper, Maureen Perrie, and E. A. Rees, eds., *Soviet History, 1917–1953: Essays in Honour of R. W. Davies* (London: Macmillan, 1995), pp. 104–7. Khlevynuk et al., eds., *Stalinskoe Politbyuro v 30-e gody.*

Between Politburo sessions decisions were taken on an almost daily basis through consultation (*opros*) of its members. As the gap between formal sessions increased, this practice was extended, though it meant that a great number of decisions would await formal approval at the next Politburo meeting. The practice of *opros* allowed Politburo members to express their views for or against particular propositions. This right to dissent appears to have been used very rarely, however; in the great majority of cases Politburo members concurred with the proposals put before them.

Politburo commissions, or as sometimes designated, joint Politburo-Sovnarkom commissions, played a key role in decision making and in drafting legislation. In some cases these were virtually permanent bodies, such as the Defense Commission, and after August 1933 the Transport Commission. A key role in shaping the country's foreign trade policy was played by the Commission for Hard Currency. A plethora of Politburo ad hoc committees were charged with processing matters, undertaking inquiries, resolving disputes, and drafting legislation.

Much more work is needed on the papers contained in the special files, on the working papers of the Politburo, and on the papers of the innumerable Politburo commissions before we can speak authoritatively about the way in which this body worked— the influence of individual Politburo members on particular policy issues and their relationship with Stalin.[12]

PARTY DEPARTMENTS

The Party's Orgburo and Secretariat were effectively under Stalin's control from 1922 on, after Stalin was elected General Secretary. These bodies in the past were seen as providing Stalin with his real power base within the central party apparatus, controlling appointments, managing organizational matters, and checking on policy implementation. The archives suggest that the role of these

12. The best and fullest account of the Politburo is O. Khlevnyuk, *Politbyuro: Mekhanizm vlast'* (Moscow, 1998).

bodies may have been exaggerated. From 1929 onward Stalin never attended their formal meetings. The conduct of the sessions of both bodies was entrusted to his lieutenants: Molotov until December 1930, and thereafter Kaganovich. Stalin's absence from these meetings, while reflecting a measure of delegated authority, also indicates clearly the extent to which he already commanded a position of unique authority. [13]

The XVI Party Congress in 1930 elected a Secretariat of five members (K. Ya. Bauman, L. M. Kaganovich, V. M. Molotov, P. P. Postyshev, I. V. Stalin) and two candidates (I. M. Moskin, N. M. Shvernik). The Orgburo consisted of eleven members and four candidates. It was led by the same team as the Secretariat. The sessions of both Orgburo and Secretariat, like those of the Politburo, were attended not only by the members of these bodies but also by members of the Politburo, the Central Committee, and the party control bodies. An attendance of some forty was normal, but in some cases as many as sixty-five are listed as being present. The Orgburo sessions from 1938 onward were chaired by Zhdanov or Malenkov.[14]

Like the Politburo, the meetings of both Secretariat and Orgburo, which in the 1920s had been held on a weekly basis, also declined sharply. The main decline, as with the Politburo, came in 1933. From then on, formal sessions of the Secretariat virtually ceased, but the Orgburo continued to hold a limited number of formal sessions through this period. When formal sessions did not take place protocols were still issued for both bodies, recording decisions that had been taken through consultation of their members.[15]

The sharp decline of the central party organs in 1933 had a number of causes. It coincided with the famine and the crisis of confidence that this created within the party. The archives give us

13. Rees, "Stalin, the Politburo, and Rail Transport Policy," p. 13, cites RGASPI, 17/113/600 to 17/114/40.

14. Ibid., p. 108.

15. Ibid., p. 107.

a fuller picture of the internal opposition groups that arose in this period—the Ryutin group, the Eismont-Tolmachev group. We now have the text of the Ryutin Platform with its scathing denunciation of Stalin from a "Leninist" perspective. External factors may also have played a contributory role, notably the threat of war with Japan in the Far East and Hitler's appointment as Chancellor of Germany in 1933. With the decline of the central party organs Stalin's personal dictatorship was consolidated. This involved also a certain streamlining of a decision-making process, which previously had often been cumbersome and slow.

Stalin was anxious to preserve the unity of his ruling group. In 1931 he confided to Kaganovich his concern regarding conflicts between leading Politburo members. Relations between Ordzhonikidze (head of the powerful industrial commissariat) and Molotov (chairman of Sovnarkom) and Kuibyshev (chairman of Gosplan) were extremely fraught. Also, Kuibyshev's alcoholism raised doubts about his ability to perform his duties. But Stalin's main fear was that such disputes if left unchecked could lead to a split in the ruling group, which, in Stalin's words, "was formed historically in the struggle with all forms of opportunism." Stalin, it appears, counted on Kaganovich to exercise some restraint on his close friend Ordzhonikidze.

Stalin at this time was also concerned with preserving the Politburo's status as the supreme decision-making body. In September 1931 he voiced alarm at the way Ordzhonikidze sought to raise matters in the Politburo with the aim of revising Sovnarkom decisions and even earlier decisions of the Politburo. He warned Kaganovich that such developments "turns the PB into an organ for rubber stamping the resolutions of [various commissariats]. It is impossible to tolerate these attempts to turn the Central Committee from a leading organ into an organ subordinate to the particular needs of individual commissariats."[16]

Stalin was also anxious to ensure that people of calibre were

16. Rees, ed., *Decision-Making in the Stalinist Command Economy*, p. 16.

retained in the central party organs, so as to ensure that their authority was not diminished. In October 1931 he objected to the suggestion that Postyshev be transferred from the Secretariat to Sovnarkom. In the summer of 1932 Stalin dropped proposals to appoint Kaganovich as general secretary of the Ukrainian Communist Party because he feared that this would seriously weaken the central party Secretariat.

HOW STALIN WORKED

A major advance in our understanding of the way in which the decision-making process operated under Stalin was provided with the publication of the diary of those attending the meetings in Stalin's private Kremlin office from 1924 until 1953. In this period Stalin met over 7,000 different people. For senior figures like Molotov the meetings were almost on a daily basis when Stalin was in Moscow. The listing of the people who attended these meetings itself provides a wealth of information, and this information remains to be fully analyzed. In the 1930s real power passed from the Politburo to these face-to-face meetings with Stalin. What is clear is that Stalin was very closely involved in decision making on a day-to-day basis. He was intimately involved in all major policy fields, although not all issues merited his attention. The diary indicates a regular work routine, of almost daily meetings lasting several hours with high-ranking officials in the party, state, economic, military, and security agencies. All the members of the Politburo were in regular attendance. The meetings from the early 1930s onward were usually held in the evenings, often lasting until the early hours of the morning.

From these meetings we have a much clearer picture of the way Stalin worked. Stalin did not rule alone. We can chart the rise and fall of the fortunes of individual leaders (the extraordinary rise of N. I. Ezhov in 1936–1938 to a position of almost second in command, the significant demise of Kaganovich after 1941). We can chart the kind of officials he met. An experiment in

1933–34 to summon republican and regional leaders on a regular basis to these meetings, normally coinciding with Central Committee plenums, quickly fell into abeyance. From 1938 to 1941 Stalin's meetings were largely with defense, military, and security leaders, and also with the directors of defense enterprises, military commanders and specialists (including scientists and inventors), and with regional NKVD operatives. Stalin did not depend solely on the advice offered by agency chiefs, but received information from officials from various levels of the hierarchy.

These meetings in Stalin's office were fundamentally different from the formal meetings of the Politburo in that they conferred on Stalin, in contrast to all his Politburo colleagues, a unique authority and aura of power. In this way he was kept informed of developments in all major policy fields. Senior officials reported directly to him, and they knew that they were liable to be called to account and required to answer personally for the institutions and policy areas for which they were responsible. Decision making became highly personalized. Through these meetings Stalin also gained direct access to lower-level officials, without having to go through any intermediate links.

A further important source of information on the operation of the political leadership in the 1930s is provided by Stalin's correspondence with his two key deputies, Molotov and Kaganovich, during the *vozhd*'s prolonged summer vacations from 1930 to 1936. This correspondence further confirms the highly personalized nature of the Stalinist system of rule.[17] Molotov and Kaganovich were Stalin's closest deputies, but they were also keen rivals. Both were capable and hard-working administrators, who contributed in large measure to the shaping of the Stalinist system. Their relationship with Stalin reflects the inner dynamics of the ruling group.

The correspondence is extremely informative. It delves into

17. Lih, Naumov, and Khlevniuk, eds., *Stalin's Letters to Molotov*; Davies et al, eds., *The Stalin-Kaganovich Letters*.

the details of policy decisions across the whole spectrum of issues. Often Stalin personally assumed responsibility for drafting legislation. Even when he was away from the capital Stalin was kept constantly informed on developments; the exchange of letters and telegrams was continuous. Indeed, it was not unusual in periods of intense activity for Stalin and Kaganovich to send each other three or four lengthy telegrams detailing policy issues, in one day. Top-secret correspondence was transported by special couriers. From 1936 onward, communication was increasingly by telephone. From this correspondence we see how Stalin was constantly involved in policy making.

Stalin up to 1936 delegated considerable powers to his Politburo colleagues, but he clearly dominated them, and even the most powerful of those colleagues sought to anticipate and comply with his wishes, and to avoid abrasive arguments. Both Molotov and Kaganovich anxiously solicited Stalin's opinion on matters great and small, constantly reassuring him that they had fully understood and complied with his orders. They sought to influence his views with evidence and argument, but they did not contradict him. They were also quick to bolster his self-esteem with flattery. Like all members of the Politburo they took their cues from Stalin; they desired his approval, they treated him with great respect, and regarded him with a certain awe—and after 1936 with fear.

THE STATE APPARATUS

The state apparatus in the 1930s was headed by the Congress of Soviets and its Central Executive Committee (TsIK)—the Soviet parliament—and by the Council of People's Commissars (Sovnarkom).[18] The system was notable for a near fusion between the ruling party, on the one hand, and the parliament and government on the other. From 1917, state institutions were effectively domi-

18. For Sovnarkom see D. H. Watson, *Molotov and Soviet Government: Sovnarkom 1930–1941* (London: Macmillan, 1996).

nated by the CPSU, although constitutionally these bodies retained a separate identity and their own distinct responsibilities. The Central Executive Committee, supposedly the chief legislative body, to which Sovnarkom was theoretically accountable, was in reality a means of according the regime a semblance of legitimacy.

The formal separation of party and government was reflected in the separation of the leadership of these institutions. Stalin became party General Secretary in 1922. A. I. Rykov replaced Lenin as chairman of Sovnarkom in 1924. In December 1930 Rykov was ousted and Molotov, who had no previous experience of government work, on Stalin's insistence, was appointed chairman of Sovnarkom. This was intended to secure a closer working relationship between the Politburo and government bodies, and to avoid the kind of conflicts that had arisen under Rykov during the struggle with the "Rightists" in 1928–29. Sovnarkom and the commissariats were charged with the task of implementing party policy. There is no evidence that Sovnarkom acted like a cabinet or operated on principles of "collective responsibility"; during the 1930s it was primarily concerned with economic, and to a certain extent social, administration. Although Sovnarkom was formally responsible for the commissariats of foreign affairs, defense, and internal affairs (including security), these key policy areas were always dealt with by the Politburo. Neither Litvinov, commissar of International Affairs, nor Yagoda, commissar of NKVD, was a member of the Politburo, but the great economic controllers (Kuibyshev, Mikoyan, and later on Kaganovich) were all leading members of the Politburo, demonstrating the primacy of economic affairs in politics for at least the first half of the 1930s. The great power wielded by the economic commissariats during the First Five-Year Plan was offset by the burgeoning power of NKVD and the Commissariat of Defense during the second half of the 1930s.

The new joint Sovnarkom–Central Committee decrees issued after 1930 symbolized the new unity of party and state bodies. They were usually signed by Molotov and Stalin, with Molotov signing first as chairman of Sovnarkom. By 1936 these decrees seem to have been discussed mainly in the Politburo, rather than in Sovnarkom. Sovnarkom was tightly controlled by the Politburo, and Molotov regularly sought approval on "sensitive" issues. The opening of the archives has revealed for the first time the huge volume of decrees issued by Sovnarkom and the Council of Labor and Defense, including a vast number of secret decrees (on this see the Davies chapter).

The Sovnarkom approved by the VI Congress of Soviets on March 18, 1931, consisted of fifteen members, including the chairman (Molotov), three deputy chairmen, and eleven other commissars. The deputy chairmen played an important role: A. A. Andreev headed the state control agency, Kuibyshev headed Gosplan, and Ya. E. Rudzutak (without portfolio) provided support to Molotov. Each of the three deputy chairmen was assigned responsibility for overseeing the work of different commissariats and state commissions and committees.

Sovnarkom had little control over its own membership. Commissars, deputy commissars, and even collegium members of the commissariats were all appointed by the Politburo. Formal meetings of Sovnarkom, which were phased with those of the Politburo and Orgburo, were attended by a large number of individuals. At the thirty-four meetings of Sovnarkom held in 1931 the numbers attending varied between twenty-one and forty-six. Sovnarkom's chief concern was implementing the annual and quarterly plans, which it discussed with monotonous regularity. Sovnarkom's plenary session paid little attention to the drafting of the Second Five-Year Plan. Here Gosplan, in consultation with the commissariats, played the main role. Stalin did not always involve himself in the details of policy making, as is shown in the drafting of the Second Five-Year Plan, the details of which were left to be worked out largely by Kuibyshev (head of Gosplan) and Molotov (head of Sovnarkom). General directives for the plan were drafted by the Politburo in consultation with leading commissars in August 1932, and by the XVII Party Conference in January 1932. The plan was approved by the XVII Party Congress in March 1934, but a further round of consultation occurred before it was finally approved by a Sovnarkom decree in November 1934.

Sovnarkom, like the Politburo, was often overloaded with petty business, which it sought to delegate to other bodies. Sovnarkom had its standing commissions, the most important of which was the Council of Labor and Defense (STO), whose leadership was identical to Sovnarkom, although the division of responsibility between Sovnarkom and STO was never precisely laid down, and the meetings of STO were phased with those of Sovnarkom. Although Stalin was a member of STO from December 1930, he never, with one single exception, attended its meetings. Attached to STO there were a number of commissions and committees (the most important of which was the Committee for Agricultural Procurements), which were more specifically concerned with the management of the economy and brought together representatives from different commissariats to resolve particular problems.

What historians now appreciate, more than ever before, is the sheer volume of work handled by the Politburo and Sovnarkom and by the individual commissariats, and the immense pressure that this placed on individuals and the implications that this carried for decision making and for the control of policy implementation.[19] Notwithstanding these problems, the policy makers in the main were well informed. Decisions were taken in full knowledge of the situation and of their wider implications. At the same time, the range of policy options considered was strongly circumscribed by ideological considerations.

Within that Stalinist system attempts to define constitutionally the respective powers of different institutions became ever more difficult. The boundaries between the political and the administrative realm were obscured. Political debate was increasingly domi-

19. See Rees, ed., *Decision-Making*, pp. 262–74.

nated by problems associated with the management and effective operation of the economy, as well as by questions of defense and internal security. The proliferation of control agencies reflected the problem of regulating relations between institutions, defining their areas of responsibility and ensuring fulfillment of their functions.

CONTROL COMMISSIONS

The Stalinist regime was obsessively concerned with the control and regulation of the activities of subordinates (on this see the chapter by Belova). In particular, the Politburo was intent on ensuring fulfillment of its directives and orders. Investigative commissions headed by Politburo and Central Committee members were regularly dispatched to trouble spots. Party instructors and inspectors performed a constant monitoring role. The Secretariat departments could carry out investigations, request materials and documents, interview commissars and officials, submit reports to higher party organs, and instruct the commissariats as to how policies should be put into effect. The Orgburo controlled appointments of government officials through the nomenklatura system. The Central Committee's specialist Industrial, Agricultural, and Transport sectors often bypassed Sovnarkom and dealt directly with the commissariats.

This system of central control was further tightened in 1933 with the establishment of the political departments (*politotdely*) in the commissariats of agriculture and rail and water transport, headed by their own Political Administrations, which were directly answerable to the party Secretariat. This was based on the model of the militarized administrative system, staffed with army and NKVD personnel, which was first developed during the civil war.

At the XVIII Party Congress in 1934, the powerful party-state control agency (Central Control Commission-Rabkrin), which Stalin had used to defeat his enemies and to shape the policies of the "revolution from above," was abolished—primarily because of its failure to ensure effective implementation of official policy during the famine crisis of 1932–33. It was replaced by a new Commission of Party Control (KPK), headed by L. M. Kaganovich, and by a new Commission of Soviet Control (KSK), headed by V. V. Kuibyshev. These bodies reported respectively to the Politburo and Sovnarkom and were charged with ensuring timely and correct implementation of official policy. The regional plenipotentiaries of KPK and KSK were appointed from the center (see again the chapter by Belova). Control within the party itself was tightened with the creation of the central Purge Commission in 1933, which in the following two years carried out a major purge of the party's ranks. In 1934 the creation of the Central Committee's Organization of Leading Party Organs (ORPO) established close oversight over the works of republican and regional party organs.

This obsessive concern with control and monitoring was symptomatic of an administrative system under enormous stress. A major cleavage in the Soviet governmental apparatus was that between the economic commissariats on the one hand and the control agencies on the other. The control agencies were often the source of radicalizing influences that led to exaggeration in policy making. The heads of the economic commissariats waged a constant struggle to limit the influence of the control organs within their institutions. With the unleashing of the terror in 1936 this institutional struggle assumed critical importance.

The problem of control was greatly increased with the vast proliferation of commissariats and regional territorial units. Beginning with just one industrial commissariat in 1932, a succession of splits and reorganizations produced a total of twenty-two industrial commissariats by 1941, the main changes coming after 1938. This was paralleled by a fragmentation of the larger territorial administrative regions (*oblasts*), in an effort to make the commissariats and regions more amenable to central directives. But the task of directing, coordinating, and monitoring the work of this vast state apparatus placed enormous strain on the central party and governmental bodies. The reorganization of Sovnarkom associated with the adoption of the Stalin Constitution of 1936 was an attempt to cope with this burden. In April 1937 STO was abolished and replaced by the Economic Council, which had subcommittees responsible for coordinating the commissariats responsible for different branches of the economy.

Although part of the work was taken over by the central party apparatus, the Politburo, Orgburo, and Secretariat could no longer perform this coordinating and controlling function. The meetings in Stalin's Kremlin office, largely given over to defense and security matters, could not perform this function either. A growing burden of administration was thus inevitably thrown onto the shoulders of Sovnarkom and the governmental apparatus. This posed the danger of isolating Stalin, as supreme leader, from some of the vital functions of government, and it was a situation that could not be allowed to continue for long.

CONCLUSIONS: THE NATURE OF THE STALINIST REGIME

The opening of the archives has made possible a much fuller account of the workings of the party and governmental apparatus in the 1930s. Some of the cherished assumptions about Stalin and his system need to be to be discarded or qualified. There is no evidence that the political leadership from 1930 onward was divided between a liberal and hard-line faction. On the contrary the leadership appears relatively united, and closely followed Stalin's lead. Stalin was never checked or thwarted by the Politburo. No evidence has yet been found to support the view that there was a conspiracy against Stalin at the XVII Party Congress. Solid evidence implicating Stalin in plotting Kirov's assassination is lacking, although there is abundant evidence to indicate that he took full advantage of the assassination to strengthen his own position.

The new material from the archives also raises questions about the way we conceptualize the Stalinist system. Many of our

past assumptions need to be rethought. The totalitarian model
was right in its emphasis on the highly centralized nature of the
political system, but it tended toward an oversimplified model of
administration. This model underestimated the difficulties of control and the sheer chaos of administration that often interfered
with the implementation of policy and produced consequences
that were often quite unforeseen. But the "revisionist" approach
of the 1980s is also shown to be inadequate, for it tended to emphasize "pluralistic" elements in the system and downplayed the
power of the center and of Stalin himself. In spite of the elements
of chaos, Stalin was able to manage this apparatus and to impose
his will in terms of policy priorities. With the opening of the archives historians face the task of developing a more sophisticated
conceptualization of the Stalinist political-administrative system
than has yet been devised.

Stalin's correspondence with Molotov and Kaganovich shows
how frankly policy issues were discussed. The private and public
discourses of the Stalinist leadership were the same. Their private
exchanges are marked by the same preoccupation with wreckers,
spies, and dissidents that appears in their public pronouncements.
This was part of the mindset of Bolshevism, shared by Stalin and
his colleagues.[20] What emerges from the correspondence is that
they discussed technical questions pertaining to policy in a surprisingly dispassionate and detached manner. On these matters
they were sometimes prepared to adjust policy in response to institutional lobbying, but when fundamental issues touching the
leadership's general policy strategy, its basic ideology, or its security were raised the response was implacable.

We now have a much clearer picture of the tone and tenor of
government: the crudity of language and expression, the cynicism
with which questions of power were discussed, the brutal way in
which issues of policy were viewed; the completely unsentimental

20. J. Arch Getty and Oleg Naumov, *The Road to Terror* (New Haven, Conn.:
Yale University Press, 1999), p. 22.

view of the usefulness of people regardless of past service.[21] We also see how, from 1929 onward, coercion was established as part of the normal functioning of the state: imprisonment, arrest, execution, deportation were used as a way of regulating the society and the apparatus, the degree of intensity calculated according to the needs and objectives of each period.

Stalin's position of supreme power did not mean that he was omniscient or that his will was carried out without question. He relied heavily on his deputies and subordinates; within their own fiefdoms, senior party, government, military, and security chiefs exercised considerable authority. To achieve the results desired, the party-state apparatus had to be constantly prodded, directed, and controlled. Major policy changes required careful management of this apparatus, and in some cases fundamental restructuring and restaffing. Frequently policies were developed as a form of campaign-collectivization, "dekulakization," grain procurement, Stakhanovism, the great purges of 1936–1938. To ensure their success these campaigns had to be organized, objectives determined, agendas set, organizations primed, the right people assigned to the key posts, and public support mobilized.[22]

In terms of organization and method, the "Great Terror" of 1936–1938 had already been anticipated in 1928–1932. The earlier purge trials show Stalin's central role in organization to rid the regime of its opponents and critics; they show the farce of political "trials" in which the Politburo had already decided the sentence in advance; the use of tactics to discredit opponents within the party, including the use of scapegoats to distract public attention, and mass mobilization and the mass promotion of new strata of personnel as a means of controlling the apparatus.

Throughout his rule Stalin dominated the policy-making proc-

21. R. W. Davies, *Soviet History in the Yeltsin Era* (London: Macmillan, 1997), chap. 12, "Stalin and His Entourage."

22. On the management of the party-state apparatus, see E. A. Rees, "Stalinism: The Primacy of Politics," in John Channon, ed., *Politics, Society, and Stalinism in the USSR* (London: Macmillan, 1998).

ess, but he never sought to monopolize decision making in a simple sense. He saw advantages in involving others in resolving policy issues, and the meetings in his Kremlin office served this purpose. Individuals could be excluded. But on key issues such as foreign, defense, and security policy Stalin sought to involve his Politburo colleagues. Not only Stalin's deputies, but individual commissars and republican and regional party bosses were expected, and required, to show initiative, but always as proof of their unquestioning loyalty to the leader. The terms in which debate was conducted were thus severely circumscribed.

But if the trappings of Politburo rule were retained throughout the Stalin era in that major policy pronouncements were made in the Politburo's name, the term "Politburo decision" should be used with great caution. Even before 1936 the Politburo effectively rubber-stamped decisions, after 1936 the Politburo existed largely only in name. To all intents and purposes, the Soviet Union already from 1933 was under Stalin's personal dictatorship. This does not mean that other leaders were unimportant, or that there was no consultation, but Stalin was the supreme authority, whom no one could contradict. There were no mechanisms whereby Stalin could be outvoted or removed from office. Thus the terror of 1936–1938 did not create the Stalin dictatorship, it only transformed an existing dictatorship into a tyranny, in which terror was a central component, where even those closest to Stalin were no longer secure, and in which key institutions and their leaders (particularly on defense and internal security matters) answered directly to Stalin.

The problems of controlling the party-state apparatus came to dominate the concerns of the political leadership. This was reflected in the progressive strengthening of the institutions of control and surveillance, especially the NKVD. The "Great Terror" of 1936–1938 was in large measure a response to the leadership's anxieties regarding the loyalty and competence of this apparatus. Stalin's role in initiating, directing, and controlling the purge was central.[23] Though the motives behind the terror remain a matter of debate, its outcome was a huge turnover in the ruling elite.[24]

The purge further strengthened Stalin's hand but in the process raised fundamental questions about the role of the Politburo and its continuing usefulness. On May 6, 1941, Molotov (already burdened with his responsibilities as People's Commissar of Foreign Affairs since his appointment in 1939) was relieved as chairman of Sovnarkom; Stalin took over the chairmanship. In the weeks preceding the German invasion, Stalin continued to use the meetings in his Kremlin office to shape policy, but he also increasingly used Sovnarkom, in place of the Politburo, as the main organizational power center. His retained his position as head of both the party and government until his death in 1953.

The new archival material makes possible comparisons between systems, particularly between the Soviet and other authoritarian regimes of the twentieth century. Stalin, in sharp contrast to Hitler, was not a "lazy dictator." The cult that surrounded Stalin, as Kershaw argues, was an accretion on the communist system, in contrast to cult of the Fuhrer, which was a fundamental component of Nazism. The Soviet ruling group was not riddled with the deep personal and institutional conflicts that characterized the Nazi regime, but factional and institutional conflicts were rife. The Soviet political system was also more streamlined. In the period up to 1939, at least, the record of the Soviet regime in its treatment of its own citizens was far worse than that of the Nazi regime. The Soviet regime's brutal treatment of its own personnel, party, state, and military officials during the Great Purges of 1936–1939 had no parallel in the history of the Nazi regime.[25]

At the heart of the Stalinist system lay a central dilemma. Hav-

23. O. Khlevnyuk, "The Motives Behind the Great Purges, 1936–38," in Cooper, Perrie, and Rees, *Soviet History, 1917–1953*, pp. 158–76.

24. Evan Mawdsley and Stephen White, *The Soviet Elite from Lenin to Gorbachev: The Central Committee and Its Members 1917–1991* (Oxford: Oxford University Press, 2000).

25. See Ian Kershaw and Moshe Lewin, eds., *Stalinism and Nazism: Dictatorships in Comparison* (Cambridge: Cambridge University Press, 1997).

ing created a highly centralized, bureaucratized party-state apparatus the system faced the danger that this apparatus would
increasingly deprive the political leadership of the ability to control and direct policy along the channels that it sought. The concentration of power in Stalin's hands, the resort to terror, the
administrative juggling with the powers of different institutions
not only represented Stalin's aspiration to increase his personal
power, it also represented a means of ensuring that the bureaucracy was kept at the service of the leadership and did not become
the master. The dramatic way in which Stalin's leadership
changed in this period, from oligarchy to dictatorship to tyranny,
needs to be related to Stalin's own aspirations and the nature of
the regime's ideology, but it also needs to be understood in relation to the wider problems of governing the Soviet state.

4

MAKING ECONOMIC POLICY

R. W. Davies

Before the archives were opened we already knew a great deal about Soviet economic policy. Eugène Zaleski meticulously examined the published sources in order to trace the relationship between plans and their outcome; he established many significant patterns.[1] David Granick and Joseph Berliner, using newspaper reports and émigré interviews, showed how factory managers, while broadly carrying out the plans of the central authorities, achieved an autonomy of action that the authorities tolerated.[2]

In a further study, Granick showed that the Soviet makers of economic policy had always sought—without much success—to incorporate an "economic accounting" subsystem within the centralized system of physical planning. In the subsystem economic incentives, including profits, were designed so as to reinforce planning in physical terms.[3] It was common ground among students

I am most grateful to Oleg Khlevnyuk for providing me with material from GARF for this article, and to the British Economic and Social Research Council for financial support (project no. R000 23 7388).

1. E. Zaleski, *Stalinist Planning for Economic Growth, 1933–1952* (Chapel Hill: University of North Carolina Press, 1980).

2. D. Granick, *Management of the Industrial Firm in the USSR* (New York: Columbia University Press, 1954); J. Berliner, *Factory and Manager in the USSR* (Cambridge, Mass.: Harvard University Press, 1957).

3. D. Granick, *Soviet Metal-Fabricating and Economic Development: Policy and Practice* (Madison: University of Wisconsin Press, 1967).

of the Soviet economy that "market (or quasi-market) elements" were essential to the operation of the system. The labor market was relatively free with the important exception of the forced-labor sector (see Khlevnyuk's chapter). The consumer had some freedom of choice in purchasing goods on the retail market. On the peasant market (the so-called "collective-farm market") prices were formed by supply and demand. These official arrangements were supplemented by various black and gray markets, the importance of which to the economy was (and still is) a matter of controversy.

The published material also provided tantalizing glimpses of attempts by economic advisers to increase the flexibility of the system by enhancing the role of prices and profits. In 1932–33 a particularly interesting development took place in the People's Commissariat of Heavy Industry. Supported by People's Commissar and Politburo member Sergo Ordzhonikidze, leading officials in the commissariat sought to make radical reforms in the price system and to abandon or significantly modify the centralized allocation of materials and machinery by introducing a kind of market for these goods. Some of Ordzhonikidze's officials, notably the journalist Birbraer, advocated even more drastic changes in the system, including the replacement of investment grants by long-term interest-bearing loans. But the reforms were abandoned and the editor of the newspaper in which Birbraer expressed his views was dismissed (we now know that the Politburo issued the dismissal order).[4]

However, without the archives many aspects of economic policy were in darkness. Nearly all the activities of some important sectors of the economy, including defense and forced labor, were classified as top secret (see the chapters by Harrison and Khlevnyuk). Moreover, most top-level decisions on the economy were

4. R. W. Davies, "The Socialist Market: A Debate in Soviet Industry, 1932–33," *Slavic Review* 42 (1984): 202–23; for the Politburo decision, see RGASPI (Russian State Archive of Contemporary History), f. 17. op. 3, d. 919, l. 2 (April 4, 1933).

classified "for official use only" or "secret." All Politburo decisions were classified as secret, and the most important were classified as the particularly secret "special files" (*osobye papki*). The
decisions of the Council of People's Commissars (Sovnarkom)
were less restricted. Between 1930 and 1941, as many as 3,990
decrees of Sovnarkom and its main economic committee were
published. We naïvely thought that this included a high proportion of the total. We now know that the total number of decrees
issued in these years was 32,415. Most of these were "for official
use only," and over 5,000 (considerably more than the total number of published decrees) were "top secret" (the equivalent of the
"special papers" of the Politburo), and were available only to a
handful of top officials.[5]

A trickle of archival files concerned with economic policy became available in the 1980s, and the trickle turned into a flood
after the fall of Communism in 1991. The "normal" Politburo
decisions have been declassified for the whole Stalin period, and
the special files up to 1934. All the decrees of Sovnarkom are
available for the whole of the 1920s and 1930s. Western and Russian historians and archivists are preparing machine-readable in-
dexes to all these materials, and to Stalin's appointments diary.
Most of the decisions are concerned with economic questions. It
will soon be possible to analyze the changing pattern of the economic decisions of the Soviet state in a degree of detail perhaps
not possible for any other country over so long a period.

In spite of its bulk, the new evidence takes us only part of the
way toward an understanding of the making of economic policy.
The proceedings as distinct from the decisions of the Politburo
and Sovnarkom were recorded only very occasionally, and disagreements almost never. However, a great deal of information
can be obtained from the correspondence between Politburo
members that is available in their personal files, and from the letters and secret telegrams exchanged between Stalin and his deputy

5. I am grateful to Derek Watson for supplying these numbers.

Kaganovich during Stalin's lengthy vacation periods in 1931–1936. Moreover, the archives of Sovnarkom, Gosplan, and other economic agencies contain numerous memoranda sent by People's Commissars and leading economic officials to the Politburo or to Stalin and Molotov.

The new information has not brought about a revolution in our understanding of the Soviet economic system. Our research today needs to draw on the work of Zaleski, Granick, and others: Some historians not familiar with this earlier work have wasted a great deal of time rediscovering the wheel. But our understanding has been modified in several important respects.

DIVISIONS AND DISAGREEMENTS IN THE POLITBURO

We now have a clearer picture of the relationship between Politburo members, and of the role of Stalin in the Politburo. The claim by Western historians to have detected major divisions about policy among the members of the Politburo cannot be sustained (see chapter by Rees).[6] Oleg Khlevnyuk has shown that the main disagreements about economic policy followed different lines. On the one hand, Politburo members responsible for major sectors of the economy sought more resources for their sector. They included Ordzhonikidze (in charge of heavy industry), Voroshilov (in charge of defense), and Kaganovich (when he was responsible for the railways). In contrast, Molotov, as chairman of Sovnarkom, and Kuibyshev, in charge of Gosplan, by virtue of their positions sought to achieve a more balanced economy and tried to restrain these demands. Stalin acted as arbiter, though on a number of occasions supported more rapid growth.

The case of investment planning clearly reveals this type of division within the Politburo. In the years 1933–1935, in spite of the clamor of industry and the other government departments for more investment, Molotov, with Stalin's support, succeeded in

6. For an example of this view, see S. Fitzpatrick, *The Russian Revolution* (Oxford: Oxford University Press, 1982), pp. 143–44.

limiting the growth of investment to moderate levels. But the Politburo decisions on the investment plan for 1936, made in the second half of 1935, were a major shift toward more ambitious planning.

On July 19 Mezhlauk, head of the State Planning Commission, proposed an extremely modest investment plan for 1936, a reduction of nearly 30 percent as compared with 1935. In a memorandum of July 26, 1935, to Stalin and to the deputy head of Sovnarkom, Mezhlauk stated that an investment plan of this size would make it possible to achieve a budget surplus of 2,000 million rubles, and to set aside a reserve of about 10,000 million rubles for price reduction.[7]

The plan was discussed at a series of conferences in the party central committee between July 21 and 28. Molotov, chairman of Sovnarkom, was away, and Stalin was the central figure. On July 21 he wrote to Molotov that Mezhlauk had that day presented a memorandum proposing that investment should amount to 19 milliard (19,000 million) rubles, but instead "I proposed a figure of 22 milliard."[8] Four days later Molotov, who was as usual on the side of caution, replied, "It is possible and necessary" to keep to the figure of 22 milliard: "I consider it extremely undesirable to increase the construction program above 22 milliard rubles. I am guided in this by the desire to strengthen the ruble and also to reduce the cost of construction."[9] But Stalin did not agree. A few days later he reported to Molotov that after a further meeting the plan had been increased to 27 milliard rubles (which would be reduced to 25 milliard if construction costs were reduced as planned):

> 22mld was not enough, and, as can be seen, could not be enough. The increase in school building (+760 mil), light industry, timber,

7. GARF (State Archive of the Russian Federation), f. 5446, op. 26, d. 66, l. 266.

8. *Pis'ma I.V. Stalina V.M. Molotovu* (Moscow: Molodaia Rossiia, 1995), pp. 249–50.

9. APRF, f. 45, op. 1, d. 769, ll. 159–60.

food industry, and local industry (+900 mln rub and more), in defense (+1 mld 100 mln), in health, on the Moscow canal project and other items (over 400 mil r) determined the physiognomy and size of the control figures for 1936.[10]

On the day on which Stalin wrote this letter, the increased plan was promulgated in a Sovnarkom decree. In the final letter in this sequence, dated August 2, Molotov replied, grudgingly accepting the fait accompli: "I would have preferred a smaller amount of capital construction, but I think that we shall cope if we put our shoulders to the wheel (*ponatuzhivshis'*) even with the approved plan of 25 mld r. . . . The possibility of increasing industrial production by 23–22% favors this outcome."[11] This was by no means the end of the matter. Further major increases were made in the plan in December 1935 and after, in response to pressure from defense, heavy industry, and the other economic commissariats. The final plan reached 35 milliard rubles.

The published version of the 1936 plan, prepared by Gosplan, made a virtue of the investment expansion imposed on Gosplan from above. A year previously, the 1935 plan stated that the "stabilization of the volume of finance for construction in comparison with 1934 corresponds to the tasks of 1935: the further strengthening of the ruble, the development of trade, and the reduction of prices."[12] But the 1936 plan proclaimed that "capital investment in 1936 alone amounts to 50% of total investment in the first three years of the second five-year plan"; "1936 is a year of the tremendous growth of construction."[13]

Thus the course of the discussion about investment reveals the efforts of the commissariats to increase investment, the struggle of Molotov as chairman of Sovnarkom and Mezhlauk as head of

10. *Pis'ma Stalina Molotovu*, p. 251.
11. APRF, f. 45, op. 1, d. 769, ll. 162–63.
12. *Narodno-khozyaistvennyi plan na 1935 god* (2d ed, Moscow, 1935), p. 301.
13. *Narodno-khozyaistvennyi plan na 1936 god* (Moscow, 1936), pp. 269, 280.

Gosplan to restrain the growth of investment, and the decisive role of Stalin.

Although there were no policy *groups* within the Politburo some of its members sought to moderate Stalin's turn to more savage policies of repression. In 1932, for example, Stalin proposed to the Politburo the notorious law of August 7, which imposed the death penalty or a minimum of ten years' imprisonment for the theft of collective-farm property, including grain ripening in the fields. Kaganovich reported in a letter to Stalin that at the Politburo an unnamed member expressed "doubts and even objections" to this proposal, and together with another member criticized other aspects of the proposed law.[14] And the archives confirm, as historians have long surmised, that in 1936 Ordzhonikidze sought, in the months before his suicide, to moderate the repressive actions by Stalin and the NKVD against industrial managers and senior officials.[15]

The above examples illustrate another important aspect of the operation of the Politburo: the role of Stalin. There is a wealth of evidence in the archives that even in the early 1930s Stalin was able to impose his own views on the Politburo. But in those years the top leaders frequently argued about economic policy at Politburo meetings. During the decade the role of the Politburo as a forum for policy arguments inexorably declined (see chapter by Rees). The Great Purge of 1936–1938 resulted in a further sharp decline in the significance of the Politburo as a collective body, and consolidated Stalin's position as a tyrant.

THE SCOPE OF POLITBURO DECISIONS

Stalin's overwhelming authority, even after the 1936–1938 purges, did not, however, mean that he personally managed every

14. This is a rough handwritten draft preserved in the Kaganovich family archives.

15. See R. W. Davies, O. Khlevnyuk, E. A. Rees, L. Kosheleva, and L. Rogovaya, eds., *The Stalin-Kaganovich Correspondence, 1931–1936* (New Haven, Conn.: Yale University Press, forthcoming).

aspect of economic policy. Like other dictators, he lacked the time, the knowledge, and the interest to behave as a universal decision maker. The archives show that, although Stalin was actively involved in a large number of Politburo decisions, he left many important matters to be settled by other members of the Politburo, or at a lower level. For example: In September 1931 he wrote to Kaganovich about an important wage reform: "I haven't read the resolution on wages in metal and coal. Tell Postyshev I am voting *for* them on trust." And in September 1933 he told Kaganovich that he did not intend to read the draft decree on a major reform of factory technical schools. More generally, Stalin and the Politburo largely left industrial projects and issues in the hands of the redoubtable Ordzhonikidze, and Stalin interfered in industry only when he thought things were going wrong, or that Ordzhonikidze was exceeding his prerogatives.

But certain issues were considered by the Politburo, and by Stalin personally, in considerable detail. Throughout 1930 to 1936, they took decisions on the grain collections and examined their progress, region by region, month by month, and even every five days. The powerful Defense Commission regularly discussed major weapons in quite specific terms; in this commission, attached jointly to the Politburo and Sovnarkom, Stalin was very active. The Politburo approved annual and quarterly economic plans, which included many specific targets for particular products, given in physical terms.

On the other hand, the allocation of products between different sectors was usually decided at a lower level, by Gosplan and the People's Commissariats (trucks and tractors were sometimes an exception). And the crucial decisions about the level of capital investment and its allocation between sectors were normally made in terms of rubles, not in terms of the labor, building materials, and capital equipment that were the physical embodiment of these monetary allocations.

PRESSURE AND PERSUASION

Stalin's power was circumscribed in other important respects. He was not immune to pressure and persuasion from Politburo members, or from society at large.

The grain collection campaigns provide an instructive illustration of the pressures brought to bear on Stalin and the Politburo and how they operated. The grain plans approved by the Politburo were designed to squeeze as much grain as possible from the peasants to feed the growing towns, and for export. Before the archives were opened, some historians believed that these grain plans, with few exceptions, were fixed magnitudes to which Stalin obstinately adhered irrespective of the size of the harvest and the sufferings of the peasants. We now know that Stalin often gave way in face of the memoranda with which regional and district party officials bombarded the Politburo. These presented the case for reducing the grain plans and supplying more food to the peasants, fiercely and in detail. A verbatim report of a plenum (plenary meeting) of the party central committee on October 31, 1931, records that at this meeting the grain collections were the subject of a sharp clash between the Moscow Politburo and regional leaders. Khataevich, party secretary of the Central Volga region, frankly stated that his region could not reach its target of 100 million puds (1.638 million tons). He complained that "the collective farmer will not eat his fill," echoing the famous remark of Vyshnegradsky, a tsarist minister of finance, that "we shall not eat our fill but we shall export." Ptukha, the Lower Volga secretary, insisted that the grain yield in his region was far lower than in the previous year. He was rudely attacked by Stalin and Molotov, but he went on to point out that grain collections had met with "considerable opposition" from collective farmers and had now virtually ceased in the region: "Like Comrade Khataevich, I must declare directly at this plenum that in view of the bad harvest resulting from the drought in the Lower Volga we cannot fulfill the plan issued to us." He requested that the plan should be reduced from 120 million puds (1.97 million tons) to 85 million, 12 million less than in the previous year.[16]

Following this unexpected stand by prominent regional secretaries, Stalin made an unprecedented proposal:

> *Stalin.* It will be necessary to call together all the secretaries of the regions collecting grain. We must agree when to meet, three or four?
>
> *Voices.* At three. At four.
>
> *Stalin.* We will finish the question in an hour or even less.
>
> *Voices.* At three.
>
> *Stalin.* At three. All secretaries of all regions collecting grain.[17]

The meeting with the regional secretaries duly took place, and at the evening session of the plenum Mikoyan, who was in charge of the grain collections, reported a substantial concession. The Politburo had listened to all the regional secretaries and had agreed to reduce the plans of some regions by 123 million puds (2,015,000 tons) and increase others by 30 million (491,000 tons).[18] The resolution presented to the plenum showed that the quotas for the two Volga regions, and for the Urals, Siberia, and Kazakhstan had been substantially reduced.[19]

In his statement Mikoyan insisted: "No further re-examinations, no discussions, every area is obliged to carry out in full the approved plan."[20] But this did not end the rebellion at the plenum. When the new quotas were read out, the secretary for Kazakhstan objected, and was sharply rebuffed by Mikoyan:

> *Goloshchekin.* In any case, I must say that 55 million [900,000 tons] is impossible.
>
> *Mikoyan.* Comrade Goloshchekin, I have read out to you an official

16. RGASPI, f. 17, op. 2, d. 484, ll. 54, 55, 55ob.

17. RGASPI, f. 17, op. 2, d. 481, l. 123; this is a typed version.

18. RGASPI, f. 17, op. 2, d. 484, l. 61.

19. The Central Volga asked for 57–58, or at best 77–78, and got 78; the Lower Volga asked for 85 and got 88.

20. RGASPI, f. 17, op. 2, d. 484, l. 61.

document, a decision of the Politburo, 55 million without rice. This is absolutely precise, and I don't know why you are confusing things.[21]

In the following year, 1932, in the course of similar disputes, a number of piecemeal Politburo decisions again reduced the grain collection plan. The initial quota for Ukraine was already lower than in 1931, and three separate Politburo decisions reduced it by a further 35 percent; it was referred to in the secret discussions about quotas as "the thrice-reduced already reduced plan." These cuts, though substantial, were insufficient to avoid the onset of severe famine in the spring of 1933. At the beginning of 1933 the Politburo insisted that no further allocations of food grain or of grain for seed would be issued to the countryside as aid or loans. But in practice, between February 7 and July 20 it issued no fewer than thirty-five separate decisions allocating small amounts of grain for food to the rural population of the distressed regions, and a further thirteen decisions allocating much larger amounts of grain for seed.[22]

Nearly all these decisions were classified as top secret in the special files, and until now have not been known to historians. This new evidence does not excuse Stalin and the Politburo from their responsibility for the terible famine of 1933, but it does show a Politburo that in making agricultural policy was harassed and somewhat uncertain as well as obstinate and repressive, and was afraid that the provision of more grain to the starving countryside would lead to starvation in the towns and the collapse of the industrialization program.

We have seen from the case of investment planning that in the nonagricultural sectors of the economy, the main centers of influence on Stalin and the Politburo were the People's Commissars, the heads of Gosplan and other government departments,

21. Ibid.
22. These developments will be described in R. W. Davies and S. G. Wheatcroft, *The Years of Hunger: Soviet Agriculture, 1931–1933* (London: Macmillan, forthcoming).

and their senior officials. Every aspect of economic policy was involved. The heads of government departments bombarded Stalin, Molotov, and the Politburo with memoranda both demanding more resources and proposing changes in the economic system.

One striking manifestation of this pressure was the stubborn struggle of the People's Commissariat for Finance and the State Bank to curb inflation and stabilize Soviet finance. Stalin himself, after a short period at the end of the 1920s when he encouraged inflation, spoke out publicly in favor of the stability of the ruble. Before the opening of the archives Western historians and economists, recognizing that the Soviet authorities paid serious attention to the need for financial stability, had examined the Soviet financial system quite thoroughly.[23] We understood that Soviet economic policy resembled the "stop-go" of Western Europe in the 1950s and 1960s. The effort to combine economic expansion and financial stability resulted in a moderate but varying rate of inflation.

But we did not appreciate the extent to which from the early 1930s onward the People's Commissariat for Finance and the State Bank had resumed an active role as stalwart defenders of sound finance, in spite of the thorough purge of financially conservative "bourgeois specialists" which had decimated these government departments in 1929–30. The story of the role of Pyatakov in the State Bank is most illuminating. Pyatakov, formerly a prominent Trotskyist and always an advocate of rapid industrialization, was appointed director of the bank in April 1929. Under his auspices a credit reform was launched which immediately resulted in a rapid expansion of the currency. He was dismissed in October 1930, and his successors switched to a policy of credit restriction.

---

23. See: A. Z. Arnold, *Banks, Credit, and Money in Soviet Russia* (New York: Columbia University Press, 1937); F. Holzman, *Soviet Taxation: The Fiscal and Monetary Problems of a Planned Economy* (Cambridge, Mass.: Harvard University Press, 1955); R. W. Davies, *The Development of the Soviet Budgetary System* (Cambridge: Cambridge University Press, 1958).

Historians assumed that his dismissal was an implicit condemnation of his inflationary policies.[24] But behind the scenes, Pyatakov, on July 19, 1930, had addressed a long memorandum to Stalin pointing out the dangers of inflation. He noted that the rate of increase in currency circulation had been accelerating in each successive year. Insisting that "we are approaching the moment when currency circulation has already entered a sick phase and cannot take on any further burden," he set out a 21-point program for containing inflation.[25] Stalin, indignant at Pyatakov's turnabout, castigated him in a letter to Molotov as a "rightist Trotskyist," but quickly adopted a number of his policy suggestions without acknowledgment. The State Bank had acted as if it had a life of its own, rapidly converting Pyatakov to its traditional policies.

In the years 1934–1936 the case for stable finance and for a greater role for prices and profits was strongly urged on the Politburo by Mar'yasin, director of the State Bank, and Veitser, people's commissar for internal trade. They were generally supported by Grin'ko, the people's commissar for finance. In 1934, Mar'yasin sent a series of memoranda to Stalin and Molotov calling for increases in retail prices that would enable the abolition of the rationing of food and consumer goods, and officials in Veitser's commissariat called for the revival of competition in retail trade, suggesting, for example, that the small bakeries that flourished before the revolution and during the 1920s should be reopened in order to encourage improved quality and variety in bread products. At the end of 1934 Stalin personally decided that bread rationing could be abolished, obviously influenced by the arguments of these commissariats. In an unpublished address to a plenum of the party central committee, he condemned low ration prices as "not a price but a gift to the working class" and insisted that as a result of the abolition of rationing "the tastes, requirements, and

24. See, e.g., R. W. Davies, *The Soviet Economy in Turmoil, 1929–1930* (London: Macmillan, 1986), p. 431.
25. RGASPI, f. 85, op. 27, d. 397, ll. 2–7.

wishes of particular areas and individual consumers will have to be taken into account by our trading organizations."[26]

The years in which the rationing of food and consumer goods was abolished, 1935 and 1936, also saw important changes in the price system within industry. In 1935 the "fixed 1926/27 prices" in which the growth of production was measured were made more realistic. From April 1, 1936, current industrial prices were drastically reformed. Most of the subsidies on the output of heavy industry were abolished, and the prices paid for its output were increased so that they were much closer to the cost of production. The files of Gosplan and the central statistical agency contain many informative documents in which these changes are thrashed out.[27]

Simultaneously, economic officials advocated more drastic reforms in the economic system. I described above the proposals by Birbraer and others, which were openly discussed in the industrial press. What we did not know before the opening of the archives was that equally radical reforms were supported by some heads of government departments. No coherent or systematic variant of the established system was proposed. As the experience with Birbraer demonstrated, such an exercise would have been castigated as right wing or counterrevolutionary. Instead, different sections of the administrative structure advocated improvements in the sphere for which they were responsible. We do not know how far, if at all, the proponents of the reform tacitly shared a common view of what kind of economic system was required, but several proposals by prominent officials were intended to strengthen the role of costs, profits, and prices in the economy, thus providing greater opportunities for economic units to take their own decisions within the framework of the national plan. The support by

26. See O. Khlevnyuk and R. W. Davies, "The End of Rationing in the Soviet Union, 1934–1935," *Europe-Asia Studies* 51 (1999): 564–76.

27. See M. Harrison, "Prices, Planners, and Producers: An Agency Problem in Soviet Industry, 1928–1950," *The Journal of Economic History* 58 (1998): 1032–62.

the People's Commissariat for Finance and the State Bank for the abolition of rationing, and the price reforms supported by Gosplan, all worked in this direction.

The most striking of the more radical reforms were proposed by Mar'yasin of the State Bank. At the beginning of 1935 he sent memoranda to Molotov urging the replacement of the universal tax on turnover by excises restricted to certain consumer goods: tobacco, vodka, kerosene, matches, sugar, salt, galoshes, and (for the time being) bread. The turnover tax on other goods would be replaced by a profits tax. This amounted to a return to the taxation arrangements of the 1920s: The goods proposed were mainly those subject to excises before 1930. Mar'yasin also proposed that "relations between wholesale and retail trading agencies should be established on the principle of commercial credit," in place of the present arrangement that all credit was centrally authorized and supplied by the State Bank.[28] This proposal also involved a partial return to the financial system of the 1920s.

These attempts to reform the system were brought to a halt by the purges of 1936–1938. In every government department a large number of senior officials were dismissed, arrested, and often executed. In the State Bank, Mar'yasin was arrested in July 1936 and was subsequently executed. The purges affected its whole staff. On July 26, 1937, Mar'yasin's successor, S. Kruglikov, in a memorandum to Stalin and Molotov, justified a drastic purge on the grounds that the staff of the bank had been appointed by Mar'yasin and his predecessors Sheinman, Pyatakov, and Kalmanovich (Sheinman was in Britain and did not return; Pyatakov had already been executed, and Kalmanovich was in prison):

> It is not merely [Kruglikov wrote] that 250 of the 1,000 staff of the board of the State Bank are to be removed: *half of the staff concerned with credit are being dismissed.* In most of the agencies con-

28. GARF, f. 5446, op. 26, d. 66, ll. 373–70 (not dated [early 1935]); ibid., ll. 25–18 (dated April 1, 1935).

cerned with credit the department heads, their deputies and the
officials directly concerned with providing credit for the main
branches of the economy are to be removed—i.e., almost the whole
basic staff of the officials of the credit agencies.

All the heads of the credit departments are to be dismissed, except two.[29]

Kruglikov was himself arrested on September 11. His successor, Grichmanov, in his turn wrote to Stalin, Molotov, and Molotov's deputy explaining that a number of Kruglikov's new
appointments had been dismissed and arrested, and would need
to be replaced.[30] In July 1938 Grichmanov was arrested—the
third director of the bank to be arrested in two years. This grim
upheaval in the personnel of the State Bank did not cease until
after the appointment of Bulganin as its director in October 1938.

The purges of 1936–1938 removed most of a generation of
talented economic officials. The new generation had a much
weaker understanding of economics and were much more inclined
to take the existing system for granted. But the impetus to reform
did not die out. G. I. Smirnov was briefly head of Gosplan from
February to October 1937 (he was then arrested); even at this
time, in the midst of the purges, he addressed a memorandum to
Sovnarkom castigating the manner in which fixed 1926/27 prices
for new kinds of output were set.[31] Even more remarkably, in
1940 the State Bank, in spite of the drastic change in its staff,
again proposed a radical credit reform. The proposals, like Mar'y-
asin's in 1935, turned on the restoration of commercial credit,
and even specifically suggested the revival of the bills of exchange
widely used in the 1920s. According to the People's Commissar
for Finance, who opposed the reform, it was supported by several
Politburo members. But Stalin personally rejected the crucial pro-

29. Ibid., d. 86, ll. 94–90.

30. Ibid., ll. 48–38 (dated October 11).

31. Ibid., ll. 3–5. A similar document was issued by the commission for 1926/
27 prices early in 1938; (see Harrison, "Prices, Planners, and Producers," pp. 1055–
56.)

posal about commercial credit as a return to a past stage, and it was duly rejected.[32]

The Soviet authorities did not, however, reject all proposals for reform in the immediate prewar years. Following a period in which far more severe laws regulating labor discipline were introduced and applied, in the months before the German invasion in June 1941 the Soviet government devoted much more attention to economic incentives and questions of profitability. These developments of 1940–41 remain to be investigated.

Even during World War II the pre-purge effort to modify the rigid structure of the economic system was resumed within the People's Commissariat for Finance. Some of the background to the currency reform of 1947 had long been known from the autobiography of Minister of Finance Zverev. Zverev, a former textile worker educated in the Soviet period, was, like Bulganin, appointed in the aftermath of the purges. According to Zverev, in December 1943 Stalin unexpectedly rang him up and talked with him for forty minutes about the future currency reform. "At this stage in the preparation of the reform, of all the staff of the People's Commissariat for Finance, I alone knew about it; I carried out all the preliminary work, including very complicated calculations."[33]

We now know from the archives that this is by no means the whole story. Zverev fails to mention that he had consulted D'yachenko, an official in the commissariat since 1929. On December 31, 1943, D'yachenko sent Zverev a 155-page typed memorandum, "Questions of Currency Reform."[34] The interest of this document is not merely that it reveals that People's Commissars

32. This is the account by the People's Commissar for Finance, A. G. Zverev, in his biography, *Zapiski ministra* (Moscow, 1973), pp. 184–86; some less important proposals were approved in spite of Zverev's opposition. The archival files on these events have not yet been traced.

33. Ibid., pp. 231–33.

34. RGAE (Russian State Archives for the Economy), f. 7733, op. 26, d. 1577, ll. 278–123. A handwritten note on the first page reads: "The top copy has been sent to A. G. Zverev."

depended on their senior officials even when they purported not
to do so, and that sometimes these officials were among the few
remaining from the pre-purge period. The document is particularly remarkable because it includes a lengthy and far-reaching
criticism of the price system, and radical proposals for its reform.[35]

A more cautious version of D'yachenko's proposals was put
into effect two years after the currency reform, in 1949–50. By
this time even more radical proposals emanating from elsewhere
in the Ministry of Finance had suffered a worse fate (People's
Commissariats were renamed Ministries in 1946). The head of the
tax department, a certain Mar'yakhin (not to be confused with
Mar'yasin), proposed a radical increase in the range of goods that
individual artisans should be permitted to manufacture and to sell
at market prices. This proposal, and the arrangements for taxing
this production, was supported by Uryupin, deputy minister of
finance, and was partly put into effect without the agreement of
the authorities above the ministerial level. But in November 1947
Mekhlis, minister of state control, notorious for his political or-
thodoxy, sent a memorandum to Stalin criticizing the Ministry for
encouraging privateers. In April 1948 Mar'yakhin was rebuked
and Uryupin received an official rebuke.[36]

One important reservation should be made about all these
efforts of senior officials to modify economic policy and the eco-

35. D'yachenko argued that the prices of capital goods should be substantially
increased and that the subsidies to these industries should be abolished: "*All* industries and *every* kind of output should make a *stable* profit." Moreover (and this
proposal went further than those made in Gosplan in the mid-1930s), the capital
stock in all branches of the economy should be revalued on the basis of these higher
prices, and the amount allocated to depreciation as part of the cost of production
should be increased accordingly. D'yachenko's proposals about the retail prices of
consumer goods were equally far-reaching, if somewhat imprecise: He called for "a
stable relation between supply and demand." The prices to the consumer of high-
quality and fashionable goods should be increased. This would avoid the situation
before the war, when "purchasers refused to buy low-grade textiles, while fine
woolen textiles . . . were sold out."

36. See the account by Julie Hessler, based on Ministry of Finance archives, in
Slavic Review 57 (1998): 525–31.

nomic system. All the memoranda I have described were circulated only to a very narrow group of persons: The principle of "need to know" was applied with great rigor. A typical memorandum by Mar'yasin would be sent only to Stalin and Molotov. If Molotov decided to circulate it more widely, the number of persons reviewing it was still greatly restricted.[37] Such memoranda were usually not distributed even to all the members of the Politburo. We do not know how far they were known to the senior staff of the State Bank or the People's Commissariat for Finance. And we have hardly begun to answer the question of how far the proposals of the regional party secretaries and the heads of government departments were influenced by pressures from society at large. But it is certain that all discussion of them was extremely restricted. This situation contrasts sharply with the very wide range of discussion about policy that was characteristic of the 1920s.

CONCLUSIONS

The study of the Soviet state and party archives enables a much fuller understanding of how policy was formed. Although Stalin's grasp on power was increasing to the point of a personal dictatorship, Stalin was influenced by others, even on the most important policy issues of the day, such as grain collections and investment. The Politburo continued to be the venue for policy debates until the mid-1930s, with Stalin as the ultimate decision maker. Moreover, bold reform proposals were made in the early and mid-1930s, and even after the Great Purge.

This account of Soviet policy making has shown the strong impetus to reform within the system, which passed on from generation to generation of Soviet officials. These reform proposals were largely withheld from public view. Many of the reform ideas of the 1930s resurfaced in the late 1950s and early 1960s, when

37. For example, a Mar'yasin memorandum of January 2, 1936, was sent on only to Kuibyshev, Chubar, Rudzutak, Mezhlauk, and Grin'ko.

the post-Stalin leadership permitted public discussion of reform. In most cases such proposals resulted in significant but rather secondary modifications to the system. In Stalin's time Stalin personally, with the acquiescence or agreement of the rest of the Politburo, blocked all major reforms. It is tempting to conclude that a more flexible political system would have led to more flexible economic policies, and a more flexible system. Others would argue that the proposed reforms would have weakened the command economy without providing a better alternative, that Stalin was right to believe that radical reforms would disrupt Soviet socialism. This is one of the major issues about the economies of the twentieth century that cannot be resolved by the archives. But the archives are providing us with rich material on which to base our judgments.

5

PROVIDING FOR DEFENSE

Mark Harrison

The Soviet Union was a relatively poor country that punched above its weight for much of the twentieth century; that is, its military power considerably exceeded that of other countries at a similar level of development. It is true that the Soviet Union, though poor, was large, and size lends obvious advantages to military effort. However, size is a source of weakness as well as of strength to poor countries; their lack of economic integration and the costs of territorial defense offer an adversary the chance to infiltrate the population or dismember the territory with relative ease. In spite of its relative poverty, the Soviet Union was able to preserve its economic and political integrity in the face of threats from adversaries that were both wealthy and large. As a result it was able to sustain the mobilization of its considerable resources and supply its armed forces with mass-produced, modernized equipment in much worse conditions than those under which the richer economies of Italy, Japan, and even Germany fell apart.

The process of supplying the Soviet military effort with the necessary finance and materials in successive stages of historical development has deposited a rich sediment of documents that is now declassified to a considerable extent, but still incompletely,

The author is grateful to the Leverhume Trust for its support of this project.

up to 1963. The documents themselves are dispersed among various archives only some of which are open to independent researchers; for example, the archives of the central government (GARF), the party (RGASPI), and the agencies of planning and supply (RGAE) are largely open, as is the military archive (RGVA) of records up to 1941, but the military archive of records after 1941 (TsAMO) and the KGB and presidential archives remain largely closed. Moreover, within each of the "open" archives many documents, files, and entire *fondy* remain classified; the extent of declassification is highly variable, declassification having been carried out relatively systematically, but still incompletely, up to 1963 only in the economic archive.

Still, the volume of documentation now available is immense, and the volume of archival research published so far, under conditions of fairly free access and uncensored publication, has done no more than sample it, with considerably more attention being paid to the Stalin period and within this to the 1930s.[1] Therefore

    1. V. T. Aniskov and A.R. Khairov, *Istoriia voenno–promyshlennogo kompleksa Rossii v regional'nom aspekte: ot nachala pervoi do okonchaniia vtoroi mirovoi voiny. Na primere Verkhnevolzh'ia* (Iaroslavl': Iaroslavskii gosudarstvennyi universitet, 1996); John Barber and Mark Harrison, eds., *The Soviet Defence–Industry Complex from Stalin to Khrushchev* (London: Macmillan, 2000); Irina Bystrova, "The Formation of the Soviet Military-Industrial Complex," Center for International Security and Arms Control: Stanford University, 1996; Irina Bystrova, "Sovetskii VPK. Teoriia, istoriia, real'nost',' " *Svobodnaia mysl'*, no. 6 (1997): 30–44; R. W. Davies, "Soviet Military Expenditure and the Armaments Industry, 1929–33: A Reconsideration," *Europe–Asia Studies* 45, (1993): 577–608; R. W. Davies and Mark Harrison, "The Soviet Military–Economic Effort Under the Second Five–Year Plan (1933–1937)," *Europe–Asia Studies* 49, (1997): 369–406; Mark Harrison, *Accounting for War: Soviet Production, Employment, and the Defence Burden, 1940–1945* (Cambridge: Cambridge University Press, 1996); G. V. Kostyrchenko, "Organizatsiia aviatsionnogo krupnoseriinogo proizvodstva", in G. S. Biushgens, ed., *Samoletostroenie v SSSR. 1917–1945 gg.*, vol. 1, *1917–1939 gg.* (Moscow: TsAGI, 1992), pp. 413–36, and "Aviatsionnaia promyshlennost' nakanune i v gody Velikoi Otechestvennoi voiny (1939–1945 gg.)," in vol. 2, *1939–1945 gg.* (Moscow: TsAGI, 1994), pp. 197–238; A. K. Kruglov, *Kak sozdavalas' atomnaia promyshlennost' v SSSR* (Moscow: TSNIIatominform, 1994); S. V. Kuvshinov and D. A. Sobolev, "Ob uchastii nemetskikh aviakonstruktorov v sozdanii reaktivnykh samoletov v SSSR," *Voprosy istorii estestvovoznanii i tekhniki*, no. 1 (1995), pp. 103–15; Lennart Samuelson, *Soviet Defence Industry Planning: Tukha-*

I do not pretend to present a comprehensive survey of "what the archives show." Rather, I shall give a few impressions of what has been added to our knowledge, concentrating on three main aspects of research:

—*Strategy and leadership:* the roles of the leaders of the armed forces and defense industry, their plans and perspectives, their collaboration and conflict, and their influence on high-level decision making

—*Numbers and rubles:* the more readily measurable dimensions of the expanding supply of defense: budgets and procurements in rubles and physical units, the number of establishments of different kinds and their outputs, their assets and personnel, and so on, including the means by which the authorities monitored this expansion

—*Value for money:* the management of defense production and innovation from day to day so as to achieve desired results from limited resources by controlling quality, effort, and value per unit of resource, revealed in decrees, plans, reports, minutes, and correspondence at every level from the minister to the workshop.

chevskii and Military–Industrial Mobilisation (Stockholm: Stockholm School of Economics, 1996); Lennart Samuelson, *Plans for Stalin's War Machine: Tukhachevskii and Military–Economic Planning, 1925–41* (London: Macmillan, 2000); N. S. Simonov, "Voenno–promyshlennyi kompleks SSSR v 20–50–e gody," *Svobodnaia mysl'*, no. 2 (1996), pp. 96–114; N. S. Simonov, *Voenno–promyshlennyi kompleks SSSR v 1920–1950–e gody: tempy ekonomicheskogo rosta, struktura, organizatsiia proizvodstva i upravlenie* (Moscow: ROSSPEN, 1996); N. S. Simonov, " 'Strengthen the Defence of the Land of the Soviets': The 1927 'War Alarm' and Its Consequences," *Europe–Asia Studies* 48 (1996): 1355–64; I. M. Savitskii, *Oboronnaia promyshlennost' Novosibirskii oblasti. Opyt poslevoennogo razvitiia (1946–1963 gg.)* (Novosibirsk: Olsib, 1996); A. N. Shcherba, *Voennaia promyshlennost' Leningrada v 20–30–e gody* (St. Petersburg: Nestor, 1999); D. A. Sobolev, *Nemetskii sled v istorii Sovetskoi aviatsii. Ob uchastii nemetskikh spetsialistov v razvitii aviastroeniia v SSSR* (Moscow: Aviantik, 1996); I. D. Spasskii, ed., *Istoriia otechestvennogo sudostroeniia*, vols. 1–5 (St. Petersburg: "Sudostroenie, 1994–96); *The Numbered Factories and Other Establishments of the Soviet Defence Industry, 1927–67: A Guide*, Part I, *Factories and Shipyards: Version 2.0* (by Julian Cooper, Keith Dexter, Mark Harrison, and Ivan Rodionov), and Part II, *Research and Design Establishments: Version 1.0* (by Keith Dexter), University of Warwick, Department of Economics [*www.warwick.ac.uk/staff/Mark.Harrison/VPK/*], 2000.

STRATEGY AND LEADERSHIP

The Burden of Defense

The archives confirm the seriousness with which the Soviet leadership considered and organized the supply of national defense. In the prewar years defense consumption grew rapidly to form a significant burden on national income. In broad terms this was understood already from Abram Bergson's computation of Soviet government and national accounts in benchmark years (1928, 1937, 1940, and so on).[2] However, the archives have significantly enlarged our knowledge of detail, including the patterns and trends across intervening periods. Most sensationally, R. W. Davies showed that published military budgets were directly falsified and understated in the period from 1931 to 1933 in order to influence the Geneva disarmament negotiations; the deceit was carried on in 1934 and 1935 so as to smooth the transition back to relatively truthful accounts in 1936.[3] A comparison of columns 1–3 of Table 1 shows the sharp increase in the share of defense outlays in Soviet national income in 1932 that this concealed; even so, in the early 1930s the defense burden remained below the level of 1913.

The same figures also show a second jump in the level of the defense burden in 1936. Davies and the present author showed that this upward shift was very difficult for industry; in particular, the leaders of industry and the armed forces jointly promoted mass production as a source of cost economies and standardization compared with existing craft methods, but had to face reluctance and resistance from craft interests in factories and prevarication at lower levels of the ministerial hierarchy. A third

2. Abram Bergson, *The Real National Income of Soviet Russia Since 1928* (Cambridge, Mass.: Harvard University Press, 1961).
3. Davies, "Soviet Military Expenditure"; Davies and Harrison, "The Soviet Military-Economic Effort"; R. W. Davies and Mark Harrison, "Defence Spending and Defence Industry in the 1930s," in Barber and Harrison, eds, *The Soviet Defence–Industry Complex*, pp. 70–72.

TABLE 1
THE SOVIET DEFENSE BURDEN, 1913 AND 1928–1944:
ALTERNATIVE MEASURES

| | Defense outlays at prevailing prices | | | Defense outlays at factor costs of 1937 | | | |
| | | | | BERGSON | | HARRISON | |
Year	*Official figures, % of net material product* 1	*Gregory and Bergson, % of GNP* 2	*Davies and Harrison, % of labor incomes* 3	*% of GNP* 4	*% of total final demand* 5	*% of GNP* 6	*% of total final demand* 7
1913	*5.9*	4.8	—	—	—	—	—
1928	3.0	2.4	—	1.3	—	—	—
1929	3.1	—	2.5	—	—	—	—
1930	3.2	—	2.5	—	—	—	—
1931	—	—	3.0	—	—	—	—
1932	*4.5–4.8*	—	5.3	—	—	—	—
1933	—	—	5.1	—	—	—	—
1934	—	—	5.0	—	—	—	—
1935	—	—	5.7	—	—	—	—
1936	—	—	8.6	—	—	—	—
1937	*7.2*	6.2	8.7	7.9	—	—	—
1938	*9.0*	—	9.7	—	—	—	—
1939	*11.9*	—	—	—	—	—	—
1940	*14.7*	13.0	18.1	17.3	—	*17*	*17*
1941	*20.5*	—	—	—	—	*28*	*28*
1942	*32.8*	—	—	—	—	*61*	*58*
1943	*29.9*	—	—	—	—	*61*	*55*
1944	*28.1*	—	—	—	44	*53*	*48*

NOTE. Figures that rely on archival documents made available since 1990 are shown in italic boldface. Defense outlays are measured on a budget basis. Net material product is GNP at factor cost, *plus* net indirect taxes, *less* capital consumption, *less* the value of final services. Labor incomes are approximated as total employment times public sector average earnings. Total final demand is GNP at factor cost *plus* net imports.

SOURCES: Col. 1: net material product in 1913 and 1937–1944 from RGAE (Rossiiskii Gosudarstvennyi Arkhiv Ekonomiki, Moscow), f. 4372, op. 95, d. 168, ll. 79–80, and in 1928–1930 from S. G. Wheatcroft and R. W. Davies, eds., *Materials for a Balance of the Soviet National Economy, 1928–1930* (Cambridge: Cambridge University Press, 1985), p. 127; defense outlays in 1913 from R. W. Davies, *The Development of the Soviet Budgetary System* (Cambridge: Cambridge University Press, 1958), p. 65, and in 1937–1944 from K. N. Plotnikov, *Ocherki istorii biudzheta sovetskogo gosudarstva* (2d ed., Moscow: Gosfinizdat; 1955) passim, adjusted where necessary to calendar year. Net material product and defense outlays in 1932 from R. W. Davies, *The Industrialization of Soviet Russia*, vol. 4, *Crisis and Progress in the Soviet Economy, 1931–1933* (London: Macmillan, 1996), p. 505.

Cols. 2, 4, and 5: 1913 calculated from Paul R. Gregory, *Russian National Income, 1885–1913* (Cambridge: Cambridge University Press, 1980), pp. 59, 252; other years from Abram Bergson, *The Real National Income of Soviet Russia Since 1928* (Cambridge, Mass.: Harvard University Press, 1961), pp. 46, 128.

Col. 3: R. W. Davies and Mark Harrison, "The Soviet Military-Economic Effort Under the Second Five-Year Plan (1933–1937)," *Europe-Asia Studies* (1997): 395.

Cols. 6 and 7: Mark Harrison, *Accounting for War: Soviet Production, Employment, and the Defence Burden, 1940–1945* (Cambridge: Cambridge University Press, 1996), p. 110.

leap was accomplished between 1938 and 1940. As a result, the achievements of the decade in terms of outcomes were very great: In 1940 there were seven times as many regular soldiers and twenty times as many items of military equipment (in units of 1937) being produced as ten years previously.

Beyond the reported scale of defense consumption, the archives have revealed the scale of resources committed annually to investment in the economy's specialized defense industries. Further, both Nikolai Simonov and Lennart Samuelson have researched the process of investment in mobilization preparedness.[4] From their work it must be supposed that by the end of the 1930s more or less every establishment and locality in the country, regardless of its peacetime role and subordination, had been given specific mobilization assignments. But it is not clear that the means were on hand to implement them, or that the particular assignments were coordinated in such a way as to contribute usefully to overall objectives.

Defense Motivations

The archives have cast new light on the motivations underlying the first plans for Soviet rearmament in the 1920s. According to Samuelson's archival study of Marshal M. N. Tukhachevsky (later chief of Red Army armament), Soviet plans to build a military-industrial complex were laid down before the so-called war scare of 1927 and in spite of the absence of any immediate military threat; at this time Tukhachevsky was already designing a "military-planning complex" in which the Red Army would participate directly in the overall allocation of resources.[5] These par-

---

4. Simonov, *Voenno–promyshlennyi kompleks SSSR v 1920–1950–e gody*, pp. 115–25; Simonov, "Mobpodgotovka: Mobilisation Planning in Interwar Industry," in Barber and Harrison, eds, *The Soviet Defence–Industry Complex*, pp. 205–22; Samuelson, *Plans for Stalin's War Machine.*

5. Samuelson, *Soviet Defence Industry Planning*; Samuelson, *Plans for Stalin's War Machine*; Lennart Samuelson, "The Red Army's Economic Objectives and Involvement in Economic Planning, 1925–1940," in Barber and Harrison, eds., *The Soviet Defence–Industry Complex*, pp. 47–69.

ticular designs were frustrated, but what is also important is that they were associated with other plans for huge investments in heavy and defense industry and in the economy's general mobilization capacity. These plans, with the long-range objective of augmenting capacity for the future production of weapons rather than immediate rearmament, were carried out.

Long-range rearmament was not aimed at countering any particular military threat, since at the time none existed, so in Samuelson's view its precise motivation remains unclear. This is not the view of Simonov, who has placed the turn to long-range rearmament in the context of the Soviet leadership's documented awareness of two things: the growing shortages and discontent associated with implementing the first plans for ambitious public-sector capital construction, and their retrospective analysis of Russian experience of World War I when the industrial mobilization of a poorly integrated agrarian economy resulted in economic collapse and civil war. Simonov concludes that, although the 1927 war scare was just a scare, with no real threat of immediate war, it was also a trigger for change. It reminded Soviet leaders that the government of an economically and militarily backward country could be undermined by international events at any moment; external difficulties would immediately give rise to internal tensions, especially between the government and the peasantry as both suppliers of food and the main source of military recruits. The possibility of such an outcome could only be eliminated by countering internal and external threats simultaneously, in other words by executing the whole Stalin package of industrialization and farm collectivization as preconditions for sustained rearmament.[6]

Both Samuelson and Simonov confirm that in the mid-1930s Soviet military-economic planning was reoriented away from abstract threats to real ones emanating from Germany and Japan.

6. Simonov, *Voenno–promyshlennyi kompleks SSSR v 1920–1950–e gody*; Simonov, "Strengthen the Defence of the Land of the Soviets"; N. S. Simonov, "The 'War Scare' of 1927 and the Birth of the Soviet Defence–Industry Complex," in Barber and Harrison, eds., *The Soviet Defence–Industry Complex*, pp. 33–46.

As a result, the pace of war production was accelerated far beyond that envisaged earlier in the decade. Samuelson has disentangled the role of Marshal Tukhachevsky in this complex process. Pressing the case for long-range rearmament in 1930, when the fate of collective agriculture and the whole industrialization program stood on a knife-edge, Tukhachevsky went too far and alienated defense minister K. E. Voroshilov, who presented him to Stalin as trying to bankrupt the country with the costs of "red militarism." Tukhachevsky lost credibility with Stalin and had to retreat to survive, but subsequently he regained Stalin's confidence and was able to continue his advance more circumspectly. For Tukhachevsky personally it finished badly: In 1937 he fell foul of an intrigue probably engineered by Voroshilov, and was arrested and executed (at the same time the whole General Staff and officer corps were savagely purged). However, the cause that he had championed prospered. In the late 1930s the pace of war production was accelerated far beyond that envisaged in the earlier 1930s and military-industrial mobilization became all-encompassing, while contingency plans for the future became more and more ambitious.

In Samuelson's view the military archives leave open the question of whether these plans were designed to support an aggressive war against Germany in the future, rather than to counter a German attack. However, the documentation assembled by Gabriel Gorodetsky in the central political, diplomatic, and military archives has surely settled this issue: Stalin was trying to head off Hitler's colonial ambitions and had no plans to conquer Europe, even though his generals sometimes entertained the idea of a preemptive strike, and attack as the best means of defense was the official military doctrine of the time.[7]

The present author's investigations confirm the huge costs of

7. Gabriel Gorodetsky, *Grand Delusion: Stalin and the German Invasion of Russia* (New Haven, Conn.: Yale University Press, 1999).

the Soviet war effort.[8] Table 1 (col. 6) shows that in 1942 and 1943, when Soviet productive capacities were most seriously affected by territorial losses and the war was at its most intense, defense outlays accounted for more than 60 percent of Soviet GNP compared with only 17 percent in 1940 at prewar prices. (The burden on the net material product at prevailing prices, col. 1, was much lower because of a huge inflation in the price of civilian goods, especially food products, at the same time as dramatic economies were achieved in the cost of weaponry.) In a comparative context the Soviet economy achieved a degree of mobilization comparable or superior to that of the other powers, including those with much wealthier economies.[9]

Why, in spite of such extensive prewar preparations, did it cost the Soviet Union so much to fight World War II? On Samuelson's assessment the military-technical preparedness of the Red Army and defense industry in 1941 was generally better than has sometimes been portrayed: no excuses there for the disastrous showing of 1941–42. Samuelson lays the blame at the door of Stalin's strategic leadership. Had there not been such secrecy in the pursuit of rearmament, the Germans might have been better informed of the Soviet Union's military-economic potential and more reluctant to launch their June 1941 invasion; Stalin's appalling decision making undid the Red Army's initial equipment and supply advantages and explains how the Germans nearly brought their invasion off.

A comparative perspective on World War II suggests, however, that the advantages of prewar rearmament tended to be

8. Harrison, *Accounting for War*. This early use of the archives to support macroeconomic research may be seen in future more as a coda to the large-scale Western quantitative assessment projects carried out in the Soviet period than as a pointer to the way in which the archives will be exploited in future. As is clear from the present survey, current research has an increasingly microeconomic orientation.

9. Mark Harrison, "The Economics of World War II: An Overview," in Mark Harrison, ed., *The Economics of World War II: Six Great Powers in International Comparison* (Cambridge: Cambridge University Press, 1998), pp. 22–25.

short-lived. There was no way of significantly smoothing the real costs of the war into the prewar or postwar periods, and the heavy wartime costs of Soviet victory are not very surprising. The only surprise is that the Soviet economy did not disintegrate completely. Based on the experience of World War I, Hitler's expectation was that, regardless of the initial size and equipment of its armed forces, a poor country like the Soviet Union would be unable to offer more than momentary resistance or supply a sustained military effort. Although Hitler's knowledge of history and economics was otherwise lamentable, in this at least he had both on his side. Those who now claim that the Soviet Union was always unstable should return to the experience of World War II and study it carefully, because in this war the Soviet Union was the *only* country to undergo a serious invasion without collapsing promptly.

Was There a Military-Industrial Complex?

Like some Russian writers, Samuelson freely uses the term "military-industrial complex."[10] Do the archives reveal a military-industrial complex in the Western sense of active collusion between military and industrial leaders to swell the national resources available to both? It is obvious without any archives that the armed forces and defense industry shared a common interest in increasing resources for military as opposed to civilian final uses. Both knew that bigger military budgets would add to defense industry resources, and more defense industry capacity would eventually enhance Soviet military power. The archives confirm that the army and heavy industry each separately pressed for additional resources at various times. But did they pursue their

10. The Russian term *voenno–promyshlennyi kompleks*, often abbreviated to VPK, is similar but not equivalent; this point is not always appreciated by writers in either English or Russian. For discussion, see John Barber, Mark Harrison, N. S. Simonov, and B. S. Starkov, "The Structure and Development of the Defence–Industry Complex," in Barber and Harrison, eds., *The Soviet Defence–Industry Complex*, pp. 23–28.

interests jointly? Evidence of collusion—for example, that military leaders were prompted or induced to press for increased allocations by industrialists—has not been found. Irina Bystrova has shown that at key moments the voice of even the armed forces was conspicuously absent.[11] When minister for the chemical industry M. G. Pervukhin fought the planning chief N. A. Voznesensky for more resources for the uranium industry after World War II, it was within a bureaucratic framework that excluded the military (the Special Committee appointed by Stalin to take charge of atomic weapons development had no armed forces representatives); when in the same period minister for armament D. F. Ustinov struggled to get more factory space for jet and rocket armament from the Moscow city administration, the dispute was settled by Stalin, not by pressure from the armed forces.

In general, the daily correspondence among industrial and defense officials, illustrated below, suggests that mutual tensions, frustrations, suspicions, and conflicts between the army and industry were endemic. The absence of collusion may be explained in terms of a prisoners' dilemma. The structure of individual incentives was such that the private gains to collusion were typically less than the gains from acting in rivalry. Once budgetary allocations were given, defense producers could win more resources and an easier life by inflating costs and relaxing standards at the expense of resources for the military, while the military could secure cheaper, better weapons by bringing direct pressure to bear on the producers. Thus, for all their complementary interests, relations between the two sides were actually characterized by irreducible conflict.

It appears that industry and army had little opportunity to act in concert, and even the influence that each could exert separately was strictly constrained by the political system in which they operated. The interests of Soviet society were already overtly identi-

11. Bystrova, "The Formation of the Soviet Military–Industrial Complex," pp. 5, 6, 10.

fied with military and defense-industry interests, but the concentration of decision making in the central party organs and the ubiquitous role of the party-state apparatus meant that military and defense-industry interests had little or no freedom of independent action. Civilian leaders from Stalin onward retained complete authority through prewar rearmament, World War II, and postwar military confrontations. The political influence of outstanding soldiers was always tenuous, from chief of Red Army armament Tukhachevsky (executed by Stalin in 1937) to air force Marshal A. A. Novikov (imprisoned by Stalin in 1946) and Marshal G. K. Zhukov (sacked first by Stalin in 1946, then by Khrushchev in 1957). If any branch of government developed an organic relationship with the defense industry at this time, it was the security organs under the leadership of the civilian minister for internal affairs and deputy prime minister L. P. Beria. Beria, like Stalin's postwar commander of ground forces N. A. Bulganin, held the military rank of marshal, but neither was a professional military man. Boris Starkov has shown from the archives that Beria shared Stalin's distrust of the professional soldiers to the point where, in the early 1950s, he even opposed handing over his newly developed nuclear weapons to the armed forces.[12]

NUMBERS AND RUBLES

Secret Figures: How Accurate Was Defense Accounting?

In February 1935 defense commissar Voroshilov complained to Ordzhonikidze, commissar for heavy industry, that the defense industry had underfulfilled the 1934 plan for military procurements.[13] The evidence supplied by his deputies responsible for artillery, aircraft, and the military budget showed that heavy industry had failed to fulfill its targets for both ruble values and

---

12. B. S. Starkov, "The Security Organs and the Defence–Industry Complex," in Barber and Harrison, eds., *The Soviet Defence–Industry Complex*, p. 265.

13. RGVA (Rossiiskii Gosudarstvennyi Voennyi Arkhiv, Moscow), f. 4, op. 14, d. 1315, ll. 144–85.

physical units of guns, shells, aircraft, and engineering and chemical equipment that should have been delivered; Voroshilov alleged heavy industry had favored allocations to civilian consumers over the needs of the army and navy. Voroshilov's deputy and chief of the artillery administration Efimov commented, "Industry, as always, is adding its orders for the NKVD, Osoaviakhim [the mass organization for civil defense], and [its own] test-firing ranges on to the figures for systems supplied to the army."

Within a few days, however, Ordzhonikidze replied that Voroshilov was simply wrong: there was no underfulfillment. Voroshilov launched an investigation into Ordzhonikidze's figures. Ordzhonikidze was vindicated in virtually all respects. The defense commissariat's financial section had wrongly counted its own orders to other suppliers as orders unfulfilled by heavy industry. Its artillery and shell administrations had failed to credit heavy industry with naval guns and ordnance received. The defense commissariat's figures for units of engineering and chemical equipment received were likewise understated. Only with aircraft procurement were Voroshilov's figures shown to be correct; industry's higher delivery figures included some aircraft delivered to Osoaviakhim and some delivered to the army in arrears from the previous year.[14]

The lessons of this episode are thus not at all what a Western reader might have imagined at the beginning of the correspondence. When it came down to it, there was no inflation of figures by industry, only a minor sleight of hand, maybe no more than a misunderstanding. When forced, the suppliers and users could

14. Humiliated and angry, Voroshilov prepared various Soviet rituals of apology and blame; oddly enough, he failed to carry any of them out. He drafted an apology to Ordzhonikidze, but on the last page he added in manuscript: "Wait. K.V[oroshilov]." His deputy chief of staff Levichev accepted prime responsibility for misleading him, although he sought to divert some blame to army chief of armament Tukhachevsky, from whose "initiative" the whole affair had sprung. Voroshilov drafted a reprimand for his chiefs of staff and of chief administrations, but again added in his own hand: "Still wait. K.V." At the end of the file, dated May 17, the formal reprimand lies today, handwritten in the top corner the words: "Give to me after holiday. K.V." RGVA, f. 4, op. 14, d. 1315, ll. 149–52, 155, 174–76, 184–85.

reconcile their accounts to the point that everyone knew precisely how many aircraft, tanks, guns, and shells had actually been produced and procured. At the same time the reconciliation was not achieved without cost: it took special effort and strong motivation to achieve. Moreover, the atmosphere was one of habitual suspicion and mutual resentment.

More generally, the archives suggest that this was a system that was relatively successful in accounting for numbers when they really mattered. Defense was one area where numbers mattered, so in the defense sector we find a variety of systems of accounting for numbers of rubles assigned and spent; numbered establishments for production and research; numbers of personnel by rank, qualification, experience, salary grade, and if necessary by name; numbers and value of weapons produced; numbers and value of research and development contracts; and so on. These systems appear to have operated with relative rigor in both peace and war. Thus the archives have conclusively refuted the conjecture that published figures for the wartime production of armament were greatly inflated by unjustified reports arising from the desire of industrial leaders to claim 100 percent plan fulfillment.[15] In the main, the published figures were based on procurements, and the army knew exactly how many weapons it was getting. When the published procurement figures for the 1930s are compared with production series now available from the archives only minor discrepancies appear, and these are typically no more serious than those disputed by Voroshilov and Ordzhonikidze in 1935.[16]

This minor dispute illustrates one weakness in the control of numbers. Numbers were not always known or held at the level

15. This was originally proposed by B. V. Sokolov, "O sootnoshenii poter' v liudiakh i voennoi tekhniki na Sovetsko–Germanskom fronte v khode Velikoi Otechestvennoi voiny," *Voprosy istorii*, no. 9 (1988), pp. 116–27. See further, Harrison, *Accounting for War*, pp. 183–84, 318n.

16. Davies and Harrison, "The Soviet Military–Economic Effort," pp. 402–6.

where they mattered. In this case the subordinates of Voroshilov's deputies knew the numbers involved precisely, but had not transmitted them upward, with the result that Voroshilov's deputies unwittingly misled him. This may exemplify a general difficulty in the control of aggregates. For example, it would have been difficult for Soviet leaders to be sure how much they were really spending on defense, although every ruble was accounted for somewhere, if only those down below had accurate knowledge as to how many rubles were being used up in defense and how many left available for civilian purposes.

The blurring of boundaries between civilian resources used for military purposes and military resources used for civilian production was a pervasive feature of the system, for three reasons. First, the specialized assembly of weapons was only the tip of the defense iceberg; defense also consumed a huge volume of "dual-purpose" final and intermediate products and services. Second, the economy's capacity for wartime mobilization was designed to be far in excess of peacetime military requirements, so that wide swaths of the civilian economy were continually engaged in mobilization plans and exercises; in order to offset the peacetime costs of maintaining this large safety factor, the reserve capacities of the specialized defense industry were also typically used to meet civilian orders. Third, the rapidity of technical change in weaponry, often unanticipated, meant that the specialized capacities designated in advance for military production were never precisely adapted to new military projects which therefore drew continually on civilian science and production facilities and personnel. At lower levels, therefore, the borderline between the civilian and military economies was both mobile and intrinsically fuzzy.

In spite of the fuzziness, the government's accounting system appears to have been capable of segregating defense rubles from civilian rubles. Within each agency flows of defense-related information were channeled separately and secretly through its "first department" or office for liaison with the security organs.[17] In the early years the problem was not so much to keep defense matters secret as to ensure that those who needed it had access to them. This was because managers and officials were too ready to use secrecy rules to turn defense-related data into private information in order to extract additional rents; for example, industrial managers tried to keep production cost statistics secret in order to retain discretion over prices and profits and prevent defense purchasers from verifying them.[18] In January 1935 deputy commissar for heavy industry G. M. Piatakov proposed to prime minister V. M. Molotov on grounds of national security that defense industry should no longer have to report its progress to the finance ministry or Gosplan's statistical administration.[19] In order to counter this tendency, the central government enacted rules to enforce the upward flow of defense information. For example, a Politburo resolution of January 1932 required that defense industry production *should* be included in the calculated totals for industry as a whole. And in March 1935, following Piatakov's proposal and a counterclaim from Gosplan's statistics branch that it was being starved of defense-industry data, Sovnarkom made limited concessions to Piatakov but still required defense industry to report both real outcomes and ruble aggregates to Gosplan in Moscow, real outcomes for civilian products only to local statistical agencies, and ruble aggregates to the Ministry of Finance.[20]

17. Simonov, *Voenno–promyshlennyi kompleks SSSR v 1920–1950-e gody*, p. 44.

18. Mark Harrison and N. S. Simonov, "Voenpriemka: Prices, Costs, and Quality Assurance in Defence Industry," in Barber and Harrison, eds., *The Soviet Defence–Industry Complex*, pp. 233–35; see further, Barber, Harrison, Simonov, and Starkov, "The Structure and Development of the Defence–Industry Complex," pp. 19–23.

19. Andrei M. Markevich, "Otraslevye narkomaty i glavki v sovetskoi ekonomike 30–ykh gg. (na primere NKTP i GUMPa)," Institute of Russian History, Russian Academy of Sciences, Moscow, 2000. Thanks to the author for permission to cite this unpublished paper.

20. Simonov, *Voenno–promyshlennyi kompleks SSSR v 1920–1950-e gody*, p. 44; Simonov, "Strengthen the Defence of the Land of the Soviets," pp. 1362, 1364 n; Markevich, "Otraslevye narkomaty i glavki."

Published Figures: Distortion versus Concealment.

Between the rise and fall of the Soviet Union much was written in the West about the Soviet practices of statistical distortion and concealment. On the whole, the defense archives have tended to vindicate two scholars, Abram Bergson and Peter Wiles. Bergson argued that distortion was typically involuntary; it resulted from the "methodological deficiencies" to be found everywhere in Soviet statistics, not "free invention," which he believed to be rare. "In the case of free invention," he wrote, "research on the Soviet economy clearly is practically ruled out at once. In the case of methodological deficiencies, there is at least a core of fact from which to start and one may hope to detect and even correct the deficiencies."[21] The methodological deficiencies of which Bergson wrote, although acknowledged rarely in public discourse and then only for a narrow expert audience, are routinely accepted and discussed in archival documents. On the other hand, the archives also suggest that once clear rules were established and lower levels forced to comply, the accounting for defense numbers and defense rubles was probably not significantly deficient.

Distortion and concealment are related because what the Soviets wished to conceal they made secret, and rarely fabricated; on the other hand, they often wished to conceal the act of concealment itself, and this could lead to new kinds of distortion. Suppression was the usual substitute for invention; Bergson described the withholding of information, which was general in the years 1938–1956, as itself "something of a testimonial to the reliability of what actually is published."[22] However, selective suppression was sometimes ineffective because partial transparency made the

21. Abram Bergson, *Soviet National Income and Product in 1937* (New York: Columbia University Press, 1953), pp. 7–9 n.

22. Bergson was encouraged in the belief that official data were not freely invented by a number of factors including a much earlier revelation from the archives—the 1941 Soviet national economic plan, captured in wartime first by the Germans, then the Americans. See Sovnarkom SSSR, Tsentral'nyi komitet VKP(b), *Gosudarstvennyi plan razvitiia narodnogo khoziaistva SSSR na 1941 god* (Baltimore: American Council of Learned Societies, 1947).

"blank spaces" more obvious and easier to fill in by guesswork or extrapolation. For example, in the spring of 1937 the heavy industry commissariat published figures for the gross output of its civilian products alone, while almost simultaneously Gosplan published the overall gross output of heavy industry, permitting anyone to compute the value of defense output as the residual. There was an alarmed reaction from within Gosplan demanding strict punishment of the responsible officials in industry.[23] A clampdown on statistical publication began from about this time and continued until the post-Stalin thaw.

The shift to selective revelation after Stalin brought new kinds of distortion directed to concealing acts of concealment. Peter Wiles described it as a policy of "minimal untruthfulness," based on the aim "to obfuscate us while serving a useful purpose to those in the know, not to lie"; he conjectured that beneath this lay the statistical authorities' "extreme reluctance to falsify totals, and strong preference for redistributing the item they wish to conceal all over the place in penny packets, under misleading subheadings."[24] The Stalin-era archives suggest that Wiles had identified this preference correctly. The authorities were usually truthful about aggregates. Bergson was right too: When selective suppression became hard to sustain, they preferred wholesale suppression to lying.

However, the archives also reveal that on rare occasions, when it served his purpose, Stalin invented freely, as in the case of the

23. Barber, Harrison, Simonov, and Starkov, "The Structure and Development of the Defence-Industry Complex," p. 21. The fears aroused were entirely justified, for an entire cohort of Western scholars made its way in the postwar period by analyzing exactly such indiscretions, whether noticed or unnoticed by the Soviet regime itself.

24. P. J. D. Wiles, "Soviet Military Finance: Especially the Weapons Write–Off, the State Reserves, the Budgetary Defence Allocation, and Defence as a Productive Service," in P. J. D. Wiles and Moshe Efrat, *The Economics of Soviet Arms (Some Probable Magnitudes)*, London School of Economics (London: STICERD, 1985), p. 6; P. J. D. Wiles, "How Soviet Defence Expenditures Fit into the National Income Accounts," in Carl G. Jacobsen, ed., *The Soviet Defence Enigma: Estimating Costs and Burden* (Oxford: Oxford University Press, 1997), pp. 59–60.

fictional defense budgets reported in 1930 to 1935 (uncovered by R. W. Davies and mentioned above). On this occasion there were for several years two sets of defense accounts, one for consumption by both the public and the broad mass of less privileged officials, and another for the Politburo alone that showed the true state of affairs. On the basis of the documents revealed so far, this episode remains exceptional.

The defense sector may have been unusual within the Soviet economy in its degree of control over numbers and rubles. Unlike users of civilian products, the army was able to subject the process of producing and acquiring weapons to intense scrutiny, and it had powerful motives for exposing falsified output claims. In the civilian economy industrial and household consumers had little or no chance to monitor production, and producers could sometimes provide incentives for purchasers to collude with exaggerated output claims. Control over defense numbers and rubles was not secured without cost, however, and the archives also show that the army had great difficulty in controlling quality, effort, and value for money in general.

VALUE FOR MONEY

The Importance of Cash Limits

The wartime archives illustrate Soviet concern about value for defense rubles.[25] The authorities continually monitored the unit costs of munitions, which fell rapidly with mass production, and pushed down weapon prices in proportion. How to charge the army for weapons imported under the United States Lend-Lease program was a special preoccupation; at the official exchange rate imported weapons were too cheap in comparison with the price level for domestically produced weapons, so the authorities levied a tariff on them to bring their prices up to the domestic level before transferring them to the army. All this was purely a matter

25. Harrison, *Accounting for War*, pp. 173–74.

of bookkeeping; it had nothing to do with the allocation of real resources, which at the time was regulated by a limited number of nonmonetary controls and was motivated solely by the impulse to record what the war was costing, even when the war was going very badly and the economy itself was in a state of meltdown.

If we turn to the defense allocations of peacetime, high-level decisions on the allocation of resources to defense in general, and military equipment in particular, were taken in rubles. In this respect decisions about military and civilian construction were no different.[26] Even if decisions were also taken that fixed the strength of the Red Army in terms of numbers of men and units of equipment, defense officials could not forget that they were constrained by cash limits. How was the defense ministry placed to get a good deal for its defense rubles? Value for money was intrinsically hard to assess in a nonmarket economy. Although Soviet military leaders were typically suspicious that their suppliers were exploiting the funding of development, production, and acquisition of weapons for some private gain, in a noncompetitive environment they had few means of subjecting this view to a market test. For a variety of reasons noncompetitive behavior characterizes the defense procurement process in all countries, including market economies such as the United States. However, in the Soviet-type system the market structure was uniquely unfavorable to competition.

The problem of value for money took different forms in production and invention. In production it was hard for the authorities to monitor the quality and quantity of producers' efforts and materials used that would determine the reliability and performance of the final product and whether or not unnecessary costs had been incurred. But there was at least a tangible product the technical specifications of which could be written down in advance. In invention there were additional layers of uncertainty and scope for deceit. Because it was impossible to specify in ad-

26. See Davies, "Making Economic Policy," chap. 4 in the present volume.

vance the outcomes of experimental work, it was inevitable that at any given time a substantial proportion of scientific resources would be devoted to exploring what would later turn out to be dead ends. A dead end from the point of view of the state was not necessarily without utility to the scientist or designer, who might happily spend millions of rubles and many years exploring them. The underlying risk in innovation was the same as in production, that public resources might be diverted to private ends, but it took a different form from producers' skiving and skimping, and could be harder and take longer to detect.

The Role of Monitoring

To control value for money in general the Soviet authorities deployed a range of monitoring and incentive mechanisms; here I shall mention only those specific to the defense sector. In production, permanent teams of "military representatives" of the defense ministry monitored the work of every establishment from within. Military inspection was less effective in innovation activities because the information asymmetry was greater, and probably increased relatively through the twentieth century: Soldiers knew relatively less about science and technology than about production compared with the professionals, and their relative ignorance rose with the advent of atomic science, aerospace, and military radioelectronics. In several fields, among which aviation provides the best example, the difficulties of monitoring could be lessened by creating rivalry among designers, which gave them stronger incentives to allocate effort toward the authorities' objectives. Over a significant period, roughly from 1937 to 1956, the burden of monitoring was increasingly shared by the security services, its intensity was raised to an unprecedented degree in penal colonies created especially for scientists and engineers to work under close guard, and the threatened penalties for failure to give useful results from innovation resources were increased to prolonged imprisonment or death; extreme penalties were made credible by the legacy of 1937. Increasingly the results of espionage abroad were used to direct and monitor innovation at home, especially in atomic weapons. For several years after 1945 a number of penal colonies were established specifically for German scientists and engineers whose work, mainly in uranium enrichment, jet propulsion, and radar, was used partly as a standard of comparison by which the security services could evaluate the work of Soviet designers, and also to a lesser extent in its own right.

How much of this account of the management of defense resources could not have been written before the opening of the archives? In a factual sense virtually nothing, but in spirit and interpretation a great deal. The reason is that before the archives our interpretation of the management of defense resources was based largely on anodyne official histories and on the accounts provided by producers and designers in biographies and memoirs and émigré interview testimony. Consider the problem as one of principal and agent. The official histories presented a version from the standpoint of the principal (say, the Politburo and defense industry leaders) which denied the existence of the problem (the divergence of the agent's interests from those of the principal). The memoirs and biographies presented a more truthful account, but from the self-interested perspective of the agent (the producers, designers, and scientists). This account was more truthful because it reported the tensions and disagreements among principals and agents as they actually occurred. But it was still biased because it tended to attribute such problems to the principals' low education, lack of trust, excessive regulation, and oppressive behavior toward those of superior culture and understanding—that is, the agents.

This bias took on an extreme form when Western historians came to write about scientific research. For example, no group of agents suffered more mistrust or misunderstanding than the atomic scientists. No group revealed a greater superiority of scientific culture and knowledge of the agent over the principal. No group was less trusted or more suspiciously scrutinized. No field of scientific activity was previously more firmly located in a matrix of worldwide contacts and correspondence (and no branch became more deeply penetrated by espionage). The atomic scientists were citizens of the world and of the Soviet Union at the same time, both patriots and cosmopolitans; they spoke their minds to the Kremlin and brought to the corridors of power the noblest perceptions of world scholarship and global community; in later life they also gave the best interviews, or wrote the most interesting memoirs. In short, they were rather like us Western historians as we wish we might have been in their shoes. And the tendency for Western historians to identify with their account became almost irresistible.[27]

The Rationality of Mistrust

What the archives tell us that we did not know before is the evidence-based rationality of the principal's mistrust. This is to be found above all in the records of the defense commissariat and general staff, which give us for the first time a full account of the principal's problem.

Defense production involved ceaseless innovation. In his classic investigation of innovation in Soviet industry, Joseph Berliner defined the traditional view of the Soviet manager deterred from innovation by high risks and low rewards.[28] In defense industry, managers made assiduous use of information biases to reduce

27. There is a vast literature on the Soviet management of scientific, research, and development resources. If I single out David Holloway's wonderful, pioneering study of *Stalin and the Bomb: The Soviet Union and Atomic Energy, 1939–1956* (New Haven, Conn.: Yale University Press, 1984), it is because it is the very best of this literature and yet expresses most perfectly the bias that I describe. An alternative view of the atomic scientists, based not on archives but on a moral–hazard approach, is advanced by Christoffer Mylde, "Dictators, Scientists and Trust: The Soviet Atomic Bomb Project, 1943–1951," University of Warwick, Department of Economics (EC319 Extended Essay in Economic History), 2000. Thanks to the author for permission to cite this unpublished paper.

28. Joseph S. Berliner, *The Innovation Decision in Soviet Industry* (Cambridge, Mass.: Harvard University Press, 1976).

risks and raise rewards. They drove hard bargains before agreeing to defense contracts in the first place, withholding consent in order to extract concessions ranging from "soft" cost limits to illegal cash advances. Once engaged, they did all they could to conceal costs and raise prices, even invoking state secrecy to withhold sensitive accounting records from the military. When subject to inspection they tried to buy the inspectors' goodwill with bonuses and services and wean them away from the loyalty the inspectors owed to the army as military officers, until they were prohibited from doing so. Although unable, in the final analysis, to prevent the inspectors from rejecting defective output, producers persisted in finding ways of making the purchaser pay for the output rejected, or else, in the case of some dual-purpose commodities, produced defective output deliberately so as to be able to redirect it to more lucrative secondary markets. Thus the apparently harsh and wasteful character of the inspection regime with its associated high levels of output both produced and rejected was simply the result of both sides maximizing their net private benefits within the rules of a noncooperative game. Moreover, by incurring these costs the authorities ultimately enabled both mass production and rapid innovation.[29]

Roughly similar conclusions may be reached with regard to the management of scientific research and development. The principal's problem revealed by the documentary record was how to allocate scarce R&D resources among the abundant opportunities presented by the population of scientists, engineers, and designers. One could think of this population as defined *ex post* by three unobservables: a distribution of talent, a distribution of motivations, and the true state of nature. The state of nature decided which projects were ultimately feasible and which would fail. The distribution of talent decided which projects would provide knowledge synergies of intrinsic worth whether or not they failed. The distribution of motivations decided the extent to which the

29. Harrison and Simonov, "Voenpriemka."

perceived self-interest of the agent was aligned with that of the principal. Where the project was feasible, as well as of intrinsic merit, and the agent's motivation was so aligned, the result was the *Katiusha* rocket mortar, the atomic bomb, and later the sputnik. Call these agents geniuses: G. E. Langemak, A. D. Sakharov, and S. P. Korolev, respectively the fathers of Soviet rocket artillery, the Soviet hydrogen bomb, and the Soviet space program. On the other hand, projects might fail for at least three reasons: because the agent's project was of scientific value but the state of nature did not allow it to succeed (call this agent, however obedient and talented, unlucky); because the agent, although obedient, lacked talent (call this agent a crackpot); and finally because the agent, whether or not talented, pursued a divergent self-interest (call this agent a fraudster). Naturally still other cases are possible but these were the most important.

Consider two stages: selection and implementation. At the *selection* stage the authorities wished to fund geniuses while denying resources to crackpots and fraudsters as well as to the merely unlucky. On a plausible interpretation of the records, the authorities were able to weed out large numbers of crackpots and untalented fraudsters at the first hurdle or after minimal outlays.[30] But it was harder to be sure of excluding talented deceivers, and impossible to exclude those necessary failures that are the price of success. In fact, selection may even have been adverse: The higher were the standards of success that the authorities set, the more likely were talented agents with a realistic view on the chances of failure to exclude themselves, leaving only crackpots and fraudsters in the game.[31]

---

30. For example, RGVA, f. 29, op. 56, d. 349, d. 354, d. 361, contains numerous military aviation projects submitted by members of the public, chiefly military men and professional engineers, to the Red Army administration for military inventions in 1934–1936, all rejected after cursory consideration or minor preliminary investigation.

31. Groucho Marx supplied the classic analogy for adverse selection: "I don't want to belong to any club that will accept me as a member" (thanks to Stephen Broadberry for the quotation). In the case of aerospace inventors the analogy is

The documents show that, in the course of *implementing* military R&D projects, the authorities also found it exceptionally difficult to monitor progress and differentiate those necessary failures attributable to bad luck from those attributable to scientific fraud. The difficulty of monitoring progress is clearly exemplified by the standard form in which bureaus and institutes reported periodically to higher authority, which did not lend itself to qualitative or value-for-rubles assessment: x number of themes under investigation, y percent of budget fulfilled, z number of prototypes built, tested, or accepted for production or into armament. The difficulty of interpreting failure may be illustrated by comparing two cases. During the 1930s the authorities invested many millions of rubles in developing two aviation propulsion technologies that eventually turned out to be dead ends: steam turbines and rockets. Eventually they wrote off the steam aviation project as a case of bad luck. In contrast, the attempt to build a rocket aircraft had more severe repercussions.

In 1937 Marshal Tukhachevsky, a leading proponent of the military applications of rocketry, was arrested and executed as a traitor. Subsequently several leading rocket specialists were arrested, including Korolev, who was accused of being a Trotskyist saboteur and sentenced to ten years' forced labor, and resources were switched away from rocket aviation to rocket artillery and jet-engine development. Among the advocates of the jet engine the demise of Tukhachevsky and Korolev was a cause for celebration.[32] To them Korolev's criminality lay in the fact that he had been wasting public funds on a pipedream of interplanetary space flight, the tangible product of which was a rocket aircraft capable of flying at no more than 140 kph for less than two minutes. Of course it could be said that they lacked foresight; they had no

---

better reversed: the fact that anyone would put themselves forward to join the inventors' club was good reason to regard them with extra suspicion.

32. For example, RGVA, f. 4, op. 14, d. 1925, ll. 17–18 (memorandum from members of the Academy of Sciences Institute of Theoretical Physics to Molotov, December 29, 1937).

inkling that this was a future hero of the Soviet Union whose work, ten years later, would turn out to be the key to national security, who after his death would have streets, an aerospace corporation, even a whole city named after him. But even the lessons of hindsight do not fully vindicate Korolev: While he was playing with rockets, the Soviet Union was approaching a catastrophic war in which the role of rocket aviation would be absolutely insignificant, and in which one fifth of the citizens whose taxes were then financing Korolev's research would fail to survive. Even if Korolev had been granted unlimited funding instead of being arrested and imprisoned, there is no chance that his work would have shown any significant return within less than a decade.

In short, the authorities found the problems of managing defense innovation extremely hard to solve. Among these problems were adverse selection and moral hazard. The solution they chose was direct repression.

I do not propose that this interpretation is sufficient; for example, it does not explain why repression was initiated at a particular moment, why the authorities came to rely on repression so exclusively, why so many were repressed, or why some were repressed and not others. The case of the rocket specialists also requires an understanding of the wider processes that provided its context. Something got out of hand in the rivalry among principals and agents in the Soviet system as a whole. Any bureaucrat might reasonably have tried to cut off Korolev's funding, but only under special circumstances would one have tried to cut off his head.

Costs of Repression

It must be added that even the resources of the security organs did not finally eliminate selection bias and opportunism in military R&D, and in some ways the repressive atmosphere made things worse. For example, the xenophobic nationalism of the late 1940s made it more difficult to replicate foreign technology even when replication would have been optimal. From the archives Nataliia Lebina describes the case of the Leningrad hydraulic engineer I. N. Voznesensky, who temporarily foisted an unworkable but "patriotic" design for uranium filtration on the first Soviet uranium enrichment plant at Sverdlovsk-44; the plant was returned to the tried American design only after costly failures and delays.[33] A similar case is found in the memoirs of the rocket specialist Boris Chertok: Korolev was able to marginalize the influence of the German rocket specialists held on Gorodomlia island by refusing collaboration with them.[34] Both cases involved Soviet innovators manipulating the nationalist atmosphere to strengthen their personal positions. Korolev was a genius and Voznesensky was a crackpot, but both behaved in such a way as to raise the cost of meeting national priorities.

Mistrust was rational, but heightened mistrust reduced innovation returns. In the terms of Bruno Frey, coercion "crowded out" the motivation and teamwork of innovation organizations.[35] In rocketry the work of the German specialists deported to the Soviet Union in 1946 was unproductive.[36] They were not trusted enough to let them anywhere near the core programs of the Soviet defense-industry complex. The mistrust shown to them destroyed their morale.[37] The costs of mistrust should not be overstated, however. It is not clear that living under a generally repressive and mistrustful state weakened the motivation of Soviet scientists and engineers; in some respects it may even have strengthened it, be-

33. Nataliia Lebina, "The Defence–Industry Complex in Leningrad (2): The Postwar Uranium Industry," in Barber and Harrison, eds, *The Soviet Defence–Industry Complex*, p. 188.

34. B. E. Chertok, "U sovetskikh raketnykh triumfov bylo nemetskoe nachalo," *Izvestiia*, March 4–10, 1992.

35. Bruno Frey, "On the Relationship Between Intrinsic and Extrinsic Work Motivation," *International Journal of Industrial Organization* 15, (1997): 427–39.

36. Mark Harrison, "New Postwar Branches (1): Rocketry," in Barber and Harrison, eds., *The Soviet Defence–Industry Complex*, pp. 144–46.

37. For the effects of the *sharashka* regime on the motivation of the German aviation specialists, see Kuvshinov and Sobolev, "Ob uchastii nemetskikh aviakonstruktorov," and Sobolev, *Nemetskii sled*, pp. 58–118.

cause it contributed to their perception of science and technology as an oasis of rationality, and of their own role as advocates of the same rationality, in a crazy world. Thus their motivation was damaged only when the mistrust and repression were applied to them professionally.[38]

In summary, the high-level suspicion of scientific personnel in the defense sector, the divide-and-rule approach to them, and the eventual descent to the penal colony, were not irrational and, if costly, were not as wantonly destructive as may have appeared. Scientists and designers were self-interested agents with their own objectives, which often diverged from those of government principals. In such cases their intrinsic motivations led them away from national objectives. As with the inspection regime in production, intense monitoring was simply the way the authorities chose to tackle the problems of selection and opportunism arising when self-interested agents maximized their net private benefits. However one evaluates their efficiency compared with other possible arrangements, such incentive mechanisms created sufficient conditions for the Red Army to be supplied with the rockets, tanks, aircraft, guns, and shells that defeated Hitler's *Wehrmacht*, and for the postwar Soviet Union to compete effectively in atomic weaponry and aerospace. For a relatively poor country, regardless of its size, this was a story of success.

CONCLUSIONS

Simplification and abstraction are essential aspects of scientific method. Correctly used, they become a powerful searchlight that illuminates the core of social reality while relegating unnecessary detail to the shadows. Social scientists have always used such methods to try to penetrate the Soviet enigma.

The challenge of the archives lies in their nearly limitless detail. Do our simplified concepts retain relevance when we come to

38. See further, Mylde, "Dictators, Scientists, and Trust."

study the everyday routines and exchanges of the Soviet bureaucracy? To what extent should they be adapted in the light of new
evidence, or should they be abandoned? From the present survey
of archival studies related to the supply of Soviet defense a few
preliminary conclusions can be outlined.

The archives show that the relationships of the leaders of the
armed forces and defense industry among each other and with
Stalin were habitually mistrustful. There is strong evidence of in-
ternecine rivalry, and little or none of coordination or collusion.
The archives confirm that higher levels exercised relatively firm
control over numbers and rubles at lower levels, although not
without effort. The archives show the mechanisms through which
the defense sector achieved both quality and quantity, but they
also confirm that there were few institutional limits on the burden
of costs that society had to shoulder in order to achieve them.
The archives suggest that defense production and innovation were
wide open to selection bias and opportunistic behavior. The monitoring and incentive systems employed to limit these were costly.
High information and transaction costs account for many aspects
of defense resource allocation that might once have been ascribed
to an irrational mentality of secretiveness and mistrust.

Above all, the archives show clearly how the game of resource
allocation was played according to Soviet rules, and then help to
dispel the notion of Soviet bureaucratic life as an impenetrable
enigma. The defense sector was one of the most successful aspects
of the Soviet system; the archives show that this success was neither miraculous nor paradoxical. It was achieved in the face of
numerous obstacles because the authorities created sufficient incentives and incurred sufficient costs to do so, and as a result en-
sured the alignment of the objectives of defense producers and
designers with their own.

6

THE ECONOMY OF THE GULAG

Oleg Khlevnyuk

After World War II a certain number of documents that the Hitlerites had taken from Soviet archives found their way to the United States. They included the plan for development of the USSR national economy for 1941 (without the secret appendixes). For a long time this document was the only archival source that allowed specialists to draw any conclusions about the economics of forced labor in the USSR.[1] Nonetheless, several specialized studies on forced labor were written in the West on the basis of various available materials. It is noteworthy that one of the first such works, the book by D. Dallin and B. Nicolaevsky, soon after its publication was translated into Russian in the research department of the USSR MVD (Ministry of Internal Affairs) and was typed up in four copies for the leadership of Soviet punitive bodies.[2] Other than this publication of four copies, not a single work on the economy of the Gulag was issued in the USSR until Gorbachev's *perestroika*. This was a completely forbidden topic for Soviet historians.

As for specific facts, the most valuable part of the first publica-

---

Translated by Steven Shabad.

1. N. Jasny, "Labour and Output in Soviet Concentration Camps," *Journal of Political Economy*, October 1951.

2. D. J. Dallin and B. P. Nicolaevsky, *Forced Labor in Soviet Russia* (New Haven, Conn.: Yale University Press, 1947). See State Archive of the Russian Federation (GARF), f. R-9414, op. 1, d. 1800.

tions both about the Gulag as a whole and about its economy was the testimony of former inmates of Stalin's camps.[3] But most of the other data (especially statistics) suffered from imprecision and, most important, could not be verified without access to the archives. In spite of the dearth of sources, historians managed to formulate a number of conclusions and hypotheses and to outline the basic directions for further study of the problem.

In brief, these conclusions and questions for the future boiled down to the following. First, the starting point of the genuinely massive use of forced labor was determined fairly precisely (the end of the 1920s), and the main stages of development of the economy of the Gulag were described in general terms. Second, in spite of disagreements regarding the number of prisoners, there was general acknowledgment that forced labor played a substantial role in the industrialization of the USSR. The relative size of the Gulag's economy and the real value to Soviet industrialization of the facilities that prisoners built remained an open question. Third, the extensive involvement of the punitive bodies in economic activity made it possible to raise the question of the relationship between the political and economic motives for the Stalinist terror. It was widely believed that the mass repressions were a direct function of the need to provide manpower for Gulag enterprises and construction projects. Fourth, there was interest in the problem of the efficiency level of forced labor in the Stalinist system. The general condemnation of the Gulag as a criminal and inhuman system did not eliminate the question of the objective reasons—including economic ones—for its proliferation. Most researchers leaned, more or less, toward the theory that the use of prisoners in the Stalinist economic system (which in essence was mobilizational and coercive) had a number of advantages that the Soviet leaders valued.

The opening of the archives, which began gradually in the late

3. The best known of these books are: A. Solzhenitsyn, *The Gulag Archipelago*, 3 vols. (New York: Harper & Row, 1973) and J. Rossi, *The Gulag Handbook* (London: Overseas Publication Interchange, 1987).

1980s and peaked in the early 1990s, radically changed the working conditions of historians of the Soviet period. Among other things, they got a chance to study the above-mentioned questions on the basis of archival materials. But to all intents and purposes the problems of the Gulag's economy remained outside the mainstream of studies of the Stalinist period, which grew over the past decade. For various reasons the majority of works on the history of the Gulag either dealt with the political aspects of the mass repressions or described individual structures of the Stalinist punitive machine, trying to determine the number of victims of the terror and conditions more precisely.[4] For the present, on the basis of the archival materials that have opened up in recent years and the first studies, we can present only a general picture of the development of the forced-labor economy during the Stalinist period.

The archives have confirmed the previously established fact that the Stalinist Gulag and its economy per se began to take shape in the early 1930s and this new stage differed substantially from the previous one. In June 1929 the Politburo approved a resolution "On the Utilization of the Labor of Criminal Prisoners." To supplement the Solovetsky camp—the only camp at the time—the resolution provided for the creation of a network of new camps in remote areas of the country for the purpose of colonizing those areas and exploiting "natural resources through the use of the labor of prisoners."[5] This decision was adopted in order to relieve the overcrowded prisons and reduce government outlays on prisoner upkeep. The initial notion was that the camps would be of modest sizes—to accommodate a total of up to 50,000 inmates.

But the adoption of the resolution on the creation of the camps (which had been in the works at least since the beginning

4. See, e.g., the basic publication *Sistema ispravitelno-trudovykh lagerei v SSSR. 1923–1960. Spravochnik* (Moscow: Zvenia, 1998).
5. Russian State Archives of Contemporary History (RGASPI), f. 17, op. 3, d. 746, ll. 2, 11.

of 1928) coincided with the first major wave of terror of the Stalin period—the so-called "dekulakization" and the forcible creation of collective farms. In the course of a few months, several hundred thousand people, primarily peasants, were arrested or sent into internal exile. Exiled peasants were placed in so-called special settlements in remote areas of the country (altogether more than 500,000 people were exiled after the first phase of this operation, before May 20, 1930). At the same time the number of prisoners in the newly created camps increased sharply—to nearly 180,000 as of January 1, 1930, which was several-fold above the limits that had been set just six months before.

The leadership of the OGPU (Unified State Political Administration) was confronted with the problem of making economic use of these several hundred thousand prisoners and special settlers. Initially there were no coherent plans in this regard. Exiled peasants were sent to work at the enterprises of other people's commissariats, mostly lumbering. Camp inmates were used at various construction projects and in the timber industry. In many instances the camps autonomously negotiated contracts with various enterprises and provided them with workers. At first the prospects for the development of the Gulag and its economy were unclear even to its leaders. For example, in April 1930 the vice chairman of the OGPU, Genrikh Yagoda, sharply criticized the camp system and proposed replacing the camps with colonizing settlements situated in the country's remote areas. Prisoners could live in these settlements with their families, in Yagoda's view, work in lumbering or other industries and keep their own personal garden plots.[6] Coming from one of the creators of the Gulag (in 1934 Yagoda would become the head of the NKVD, the People's Commissariat of Internal Affairs, which was created to replace the OGPU), such liberal projects suggested that even the country's top leadership initially had no definite notions about the significance of the camps and the economic utilization of inmates.

6. GARF, f. R-9479, op. 1, d. 3, ll. 23–24.

The evolution of these notions was strongly influenced by the Gulag's first major project, the White Sea–Baltic Canal (BBK), construction of which began in the second half of 1930.[7] This complex transport system, which linked the Baltic and White Seas, was built in a record time of two years. During certain periods more than 100,000 prisoners were deployed in the construction. For the first time the camp economy demonstrated its "advantages" in practice: the rapid concentration of substantial contingents of manpower in the required location, the opportunity to exploit prisoners in any conditions, without considering casualties. Methods of organizing the Gulag's major economic projects were refined at the BBK, and Chekist leadership personnel gained experience. New assignments were a logical outgrowth of this. In April 1932 a camp was established on the Kolyma, where gold prospecting and mining were developed; in October 1932 the construction of a canal linking the Volga with the Moskva River and the construction of the Baikal-Amur Mainline in the Far East (BAM) were turned over to the OGPU; in November 1932 the OGPU formed the Ukhta-Pechora Trust for the purpose of organizing coal and oil production and the development of other resources in the Pechora Basin. Prisoners and administrators who became available after completion of the BBK were transferred to the Volga-Moskva Canal.

These decisions shaped the structure of the Gulag's economy, which existed and developed right up until the mid-1950s. The nucleus of this system was large-scale projects, primarily construction that required continual infusions of manpower. A second segment of prisons (its proportions varied with the period) were used at other, less urgent projects.

Yet for all the importance of the economic assignments that were issued to the camps, camp inmates were a minority in the Soviet penal system (which, in addition to camps, included special

7. See L. Auerbach et al., *The White Sea Canal*, ed. M. Gorky et al. (London: John Lane, 1935).

settlements, colonies, and prisons). As of January 1, 1933, the camps housed 334,000 inmates, while 1,142,000 people lived in special settlements. In late 1932 and early 1933 the OGPU leadership secured the government's approval of new plans for development of the Gulag. These plans called for the special settlements in particular (they were renamed at the time as labor settlements) to be turned into the foundation of the Gulag. Only the most dangerous prisoners, with the longest sentences, were to be sent to the camps. The plan was to increase the contingents in the labor settlements to more than 3 million people, literally within a year. These numbers were subsequently reduced to 2 million, and the number of camp inmates was to stabilize at the 300,000 mark or even drop.

These plans reflected intentions that the OGPU leadership indicated as early as 1930. Their implementation could bring about a drastic change in the nature of the Gulag's economy. The fact that the bulk of the repressed individuals were placed in labor settlements suggested that they would be utilized primarily at projects in populated locations—mostly in agriculture and lumbering and in the development of other resources in the country's remote areas. But the plans to create an enormous network of labor settlements collapsed. The state did not have enough resources to organize the settlements, especially during the dreadful famine that peaked precisely in 1933.

By the end of 1933 the camps had become firmly established as the principal component of the Gulag. Camp manpower, accordingly, was the basis of the forced-labor economy. By the beginning of 1935 more than 150,000 camp inmates were building BAM, and 196,000 were building the Moskva-Volga Canal. The White Sea–Baltic project—the system of transport and industrial enterprises concentrated around the BBK—employed 71,000 prisoners. A total of 21,000 inmates from the Ukhta-Pechora camp were extracting oil and coal. The Far Eastern camps (60,000 inmates) were building railroads, a shipyard in Komsomolsk-on-Amur, mining coal, and so on. The 63,000 inmates from the Sibe-

rian camp were building railroads and carrying out projects for
metallurgical and other enterprises. At the Svir camp, 43,000 inmates were procuring lumber and firewood for Leningrad, while
35,000 inmates of the Temnikovo camp were performing similar
jobs for Moscow. The Karaganda and Central Asian camps
(about 26,000 inmates each) specialized in agriculture, but they
also served industrial enterprises and construction projects.[8] In
the mid-1930s the Dalstroi (Far Eastern Construction) Trust
(36,000 inmates in January 1935) was rapidly building up the
mining of gold. In the first six years of operation (1928–1933),
1,937 kg of gold was obtained on the Kolyma; in 1934 there was
a quantum leap: during the 1934–1936 period Dalstroi produced
more than 53 tons of gold. In 1937 a plan was assigned—and
fulfilled—for 48 tons of gold, which was about one-third of the
country's gold production.

Dalstroi's successes reflected, on the whole, the comparatively
favorable situation in the Gulag economy during this period.
Though the number of prisoners remained stable, the production
and volume of major projects carried out by the camps increased.
In June 1935 the Gulag was assigned the priority construction of
the Norilsk Nickel Integrated Plant (which to this day is one of the
largest enterprises in Russia). The NKVD used substantial capital
investments in carrying out construction projects for the Committee of Reserves (warehouses for storage of reserve state stocks of
foodstuffs and industrial goods). In 1936 a special administration
that handled highway construction was transferred to NKVD authority.

The relatively successful development of the forced-labor
economy was interrupted by the Great Terror—the mass repressions of 1937–38. Between January 1, 1937, and January 1, 1938,
the population of the camps and colonies rose from 1.2 million to
1.7 million. On January 1, 1939, there were 350,000 people in

---

8. GARF, f. R-5446, op. 16a, d. 1310, ll. 13–14; *Ekonomika GULAGa i ego
rol v razvitii strany v 30-ye gody. Sbornik dokumentov*, compiled by M. I. Khlusov.
(Moscow: RAN, 1998), pp. 35–39.

prisons, and about 1 million people were living in labor settlements. But in spite of this formidable increase in the prisoner population, the Gulag economy was going through a severe crisis. The NKVD leadership, preoccupied with carrying out the mass repressions, was not very interested in economic problems. Enterprises under NKVD authority were disorganized by the arrests of their directors, by mass executions, and by the sharp increase in the mortality rate and physical exhaustion of camp inmates. For the first time in several years the NKVD was falling far short of fulfilling its economic plans.

The situation that the Great Terror produced in the Gulag was the most graphic evidence that the political motives for the Terror took absolute priority over economic ones. The critical condition of the camps and the impossibility of making economic use of hundreds of thousands of additional prisoners were an important reason for the unprecedented number of death sentences: Between August 1937 and November 1938, according to official data, almost 700,000 people were executed. A significant portion of them, the lists of those executed show, were able-bodied men, highly qualified specialists and workers, who were constantly in short supply at NKVD projects. The main purpose of the Great Terror was declared at the very outset to be the physical annihilation of "enemies," rather than their use as "cheap" labor. It should also be pointed out that not a single document before, during, or after the Great Terror recorded any proposals by the OGPU-NKVD leadership that additional repressions be carried out in order to replenish the prisoner shortage. There is no indication in the archives of a direct link between the Terror (in terms of the numbers and qualifications of the individuals repressed) and the economic needs of the OGPU-NKVD.

The NKVD economy stabilized somewhat and then grew between 1939 and early 1941 as the Terror abated significantly. This economic growth was achieved through the "utilization of internal reserves"—intensified exploitation of prisoners, harsher punishments for failure to fulfill plans, some adjustments in the management of the camps, and so on. After World War II began, the Soviet government feverishly and hurriedly adopted numerous resolutions on the construction of military enterprises and facilities. A large portion of these plans was assigned to the NKVD. The most massive effort during this 1940 period was the railroad construction in the Far East and the northern part of the European USSR. NKVD hydraulic-engineering projects accounted for the second-largest volume: canals (specifically, the Volga-Baltic and Northern Dvina waterways, which linked the Baltic Sea and the White Sea with the Caspian), hydroelectric stations, and ports. The NKVD's nonferrous metallurgy surged sharply during the prewar years: There were increases in the production of gold, nickel (the Norilsk integrated plant and the Seronikel [Nickel Sulfide] integrated plant in Murmansk Province), tin, and copper (Dzhezkazgan integrated plant). The NKVD played a substantial role in the program to increase aluminum and magnesium production, adopted in October 1940.

In addition, prisoners set up new oil installations in the European North and built hydrolysis, sulfite-liquor, and aircraft plants, roads, and many other facilities. As a result, the NKVD's originally approved plan for major projects in 1940 was surpassed by 1.1 billion rubles and reached 4.5 billion rubles, and by the beginning of March 1941 the volume of major projects that the NKVD was to carry out in 1941 had reached a huge number—7.6 billion rubles (including capital investments that came under the ceilings of other people's commissariats).[9] But the transfer of new industrial enterprises and construction projects to the NKVD continued even after this, right up until the German invasion in June 1941. The most significant assignment, received by the people's commissariat on March 24, 1941, was to build and renovate 251 airfields for the People's Commissariat of Defense in 1941. To fulfill this super-urgent and top-priority order, the

9. GARF, f. R-5446, op. 24a, d. 4, l. 59; GARF, f. R-5446, op. 25a, d. 7181, l. 60.

NKVD had to allocate 400,000 prisoners, and the People's Commissariat of Defense had to form 100 construction battalions of
1,000 men each. But the outbreak of war soon interrupted these
projects.

The NKVD sector's share in the Soviet economy varied with
the industry. The people's commissariat played a significant role
in the production of nonferrous metals. In 1940 it produced 80
tons of gold at Dalstroi, and the 1941 plan was increased to 85
tons.[10] As a result of the transfer of a large number of new enterprises, the 1941 plan called for the NKVD to provide 9,300 of the
17,200 tons of nickel produced in the country, 1,200 of the 1,600
tons of molybdenum concentrate, 20 of the 150 tons of cobalt,
1,200 of the 3,220 tons of tungsten concentrate, and a substantial
quantity of tin and chromite ore.[11] Before the war the NKVD accounted for nearly 13 percent of all the lumber production in the
USSR.[12] The Gulag did not play a significant role in other industries. Agriculture at the camps and labor settlements was also in-
substantial; it was designed chiefly to meet the needs of the Gulag
itself.

In terms of meeting the needs of industry, the prisoners' labor
could hardly be called irreplaceable. Even though the Gulag's
lumber production was considerable in quantity, it was still a supplement to the enterprises of the People's Commissariat of the
Timber Industry. New lumber camps were set up more as an ap-
pendage of the punitive system than of the economic one; they
were established in connection with the mass operations of
1937–38 as urgent facilities for new prisoners. The camps did not
work well, and some of them were soon eliminated altogether.
The number of prisoners employed in nonferrous metallurgy and
the mining industry was not very large. The Northeast camp,
which served Dalstroi, held up to 50,000 people in the first half
of the 1930s, and only before the war did their numbers substan-

10. GARF, f. R-5446, op. 25a, d. 7184, ll. 101–2.
11. GARF, f. R-5446, op. 25a, d. 7181, l. 6; op. 1, d. 176, l. 268; d. 177, l. 9.
12. *Ekonomika GULAGa*, p. 141.

tially increase (to 180,000 on January 1, 1941). Units of the Main Administration of Camps of Mining and Metallurgical Enterprises, which served integrated nonferrous metallurgical plants, held 55,000 prisoners before the war.[13] The NKVD's other industrial enterprises did not play any significant role in the country's industrialization: A sizable proportion of the prisoners were actually engaged in supporting the Gulag system itself (making clothes, shoes, and other goods for the camps, construction inside the camp, subsidiary agricultural facilities, and so on).

The importance of forced labor in capital construction projects was indeed unique. In cost terms, the volume of capital projects performed by the NKVD on the eve of the war amounted to about 13–14 percent of the total volume of capital projects. It should be noted that we do not know the share of construction in this capital investment, but these NKVD projects were priorities and were built under extremely tight deadlines and, as a rule, in arduous climatic conditions. As the literature has repeatedly pointed out, in the Stalinist economic system the camps were the most convenient method for rapidly deploying hundreds of thousands of workers at such projects. Yet it is also fair to ask this question: How essential were these projects themselves, which prisoners built at the cost of such incredible casualties? The archival sources that have opened up are making it possible to begin researching this fundamental problem.

A number of important observations on this subject have been made in reference to the White Sea–Baltic Canal, the symbol of the OGPU's construction industry in the early 1930s. The decision to build the canal, which largely predetermined the direction of development of Stalin's Gulag, resulted from the interplay of two factors. First, Stalin was convinced of the military-strategic and economic importance of such an installation and, in spite of objections from not only the "rightwing" chairman of the government, Aleksei Rykov, but also from his loyal associate Molotov,

13. *Sistema ispravitelno-trudovykh lagerei v SSSR. Spravochnik*, p. 108.

insisted that the relevant plans be adopted.[14] Documents substantiating the necessity of the BBK construction said it would make it possible to ensure the defense of a considerable part of the USSR's seacoast and the protection of fisheries and internal commercial routes by "transferring from the Baltic to the White Sea submarines and surface torpedo ships and cruisers." The plans for the national economy were extensive: to create a far-flung transportation network—from the Arctic Ocean to the Black Sea (after completion of the Volga-Don project)—to secure sources of cheap water energy, and to utilize the resources of the North, etc.[15]

Second, even with such imposing support, the canal construction was unlikely to have been undertaken if the OGPU had not had a large number of prisoners who appeared as a result of the mass operations against the "kulaks." The planned allocation of 140,000 prisoners for the BBK eliminated the extremely serious problem of using the camps' growing populations for labor purposes and opened up vast opportunities for the OGPU in terms of economic activity.

The results of this construction, however, were so much more modest than the originally announced intentions that the economic and military-strategic necessity of the whole project must be questioned. Because the shallow depth of the canal allowed the passage of only small surface ships and submarines (and then with enormous problems), it had only a limited capability of transporting national-economic cargoes. These problems were quickly recognized, and right after the BBK was opened for operation, plans began to be discussed for the construction of a second line of locks and for deepening and widening it. These plans were never carried out. Therefore, as a present-day researcher proves on the basis of numerous facts, the canal "remained a costly monument to the

14. See L. T. Lih, O. V. Naumov, and O. V. Khlevniuk, eds., *Stalin's Letters to Molotov. 1925–1936* (New Haven, Conn.: Yale University Press, 1995), p. 212.

15. GARF, f. R-9414, op. 1, d. 1806, l. 1 (the memorandum "O sooruzhenii Baltiiskogo-Belomorskogo puti," prepared to support a government draft resolution on construction of the canal).

mismanagement of the Soviet system": "The canal's value to the region's economic development, as soon became clear, was minor. And strategically the waterway's value was negligible."[16] In 1940, the canal was used to 44 percent of its capacity; in 1950, 20 percent.[17] Moreover, most of the cargoes that were transported through the BBK before the war belonged to enterprises situated in its zone; that is, the canal was primarily a route of local significance.

A researcher on another major construction project managed by the OGPU-NKVD, the Baikal-Amur Mainline, comes to similarly skeptical conclusions.[18] This was one of the largest projects: At the beginning of 1938 there were more than 200,000 prisoners in Bamlag (BAM camp), and a few months later it served as the basis for several new camps.[19] Notwithstanding the considerable material resources and manpower invested in this railroad and the numerous casualties among the prisoners, the actual results of the construction were meager. The mainline was not completed by the slated deadline. The sections of it that were actually put into operation were of no substantial value.

The BAM (and railroad construction as a whole) were a typical example of the wastefulness of the Stalinist system of mobilizing forced labor. The disorganized construction of many railroads without the necessary feasibility study led to the dissipation of enormous resources. By 1938 the length of railroads on which construction had started but had been suspended was approaching 5,000 km (not counting railroads that had been completed but were unused or partly used because they were unneeded).[20] Meanwhile, the total increase in the USSR's railroad system between 1933 and 1939 amounted to a mere 4,500 km. A consider-

16. See Yu. Kilin, *Karelia v politike sovetskogo gosudarstva. 1920–1941* (Petrozavodsk, 1999), pp. 122–27.

17. GARF, f. R-5446, op. 81b, d. 6645, l. 52.

18. O. P. Yelantseva, "BAM: pervoye desyatiletiye," in *Otechestvennaya Istoria*, no. 6 (1994): pp. 89–103.

19. *Sistema ispravitelno-trudovykh lagerei SSSR. Spravochnik*, pp. 153–54.

20. Yelantseva, "BAM," p. 102.

able portion of the "dead railroads" was built at the cost of many prisoners' lives.

A similar fate befell other Gulag projects. In September 1940, for example, a resolution was adopted to suspend the construction of the Kuibyshev hydraulic engineering system, which had been started in 1937.[21] The government attributed the decision to "the lack of available manpower" to perform work at an ambitious new project—the construction of the Volga-Baltic and Northern Dvina water system. At the time of the suspension, an enormous sum had already been spent on the Kuibyshev system— 126.7 million rubles[22]—and between 30,000 and 40,000 prisoners had been deployed at the Samara camp, which had been serving the project.[23]

It is important to stress that no special studies have so far been done on the dimensions of incomplete or useless construction done by the OGPU-NKVD. The individual examples cited at least show that the results of the camp economy's activities cannot be evaluated on the basis of the amount of capital investments formally spent. Moreover, the sizable forced-labor economy fostered waste and low yields on capital investments, which were endemic to the Soviet economy as a whole. The large contingents of "cheap" and mobile camp labor made it possible easily to adopt plans for accelerated construction of major projects without serious economic or technical calculations, and then, with equal ease, to scrap projects that had been started and transfer prisoners to new ones. Suffice it to say that a considerable portion of the NKVD's priority projects were funded without plans or estimates, on the basis of actual expenditures.

The OGPU-NKVD leadership itself, understandably, preferred to emphasize the efficiency and importance of the Gulag

21. Resolution of the USSR Sovnarkom and the Central Committee of the All-Russian Communist Party (Bolsheviks) dated September 24, 1940 (GARF, f. R-5446, op. 1, d. 73, l. 212), approved by the Politburo on September 23 (RGASPI, f. 17, op. 3, d. 1027, l. 75).

22. GARF, f. R-5446, op. 81b, d. 6691, l. 69.

23. *Sistema ispravitelno-trudovykh lagerei SSSR. Spravochnik*, pp. 370–71.

economy. In a message to the government in May 1933, Z. A. Almazov, assistant director of Dalstroi (a few months later he would be given a second, concurrent job, the high-ranking position of assistant director of the Gulag), wrote: "Supporting one man in the fields [the Kolyma gold fields—Ed.] for one year requires goods with a gross weight of about 1 ton (including building materials); one man produces 1 kilogram of metal per year."[24] In a memorandum addressed to Stalin in November 1935, Yagoda promised that the NKVD would build roads at an average of 50,000 rubles less per kilometer than the civilian people's commissariats had been building them to that point; Yagoda attributed this to the lower cost of maintaining the administrative apparatus and to the high production norms that had been set at the NKVD.[25] The cost of mining gold and tin at NKVD projects was lower. In 1939, for example, the government set an accounting price of 6.9 rubles for one gram of gold (compared with 5.2 rubles in previous years), whereas the price at enterprises of the People's Commissariat of Nonferrous Metallurgy varied from 15.3 to 16.7 rubles. Similar prices for a ton of tin produced by Dalstroi and the People's Commissariat of Nonferrous Metallurgy were 40.8 and 60.2 rubles, respectively.[26]

Yet even if one puts aside the destructive humanitarian and moral consequences of the Terror, many factors suggest that forced labor was more a heavy overhead expense for the economy than a source of profit, albeit immoral.

The mass deportation of kulaks to remote regions of the country was obviously a losing proposition, even in purely economic terms. For example, according to official estimates, between 1930 and 1932 the state spent 250 million rubles on moving and setting up the kulaks, an average of 1,000 rubles per farm, whereas the value of the confiscated property was about 560 rubles. The special settlers' farms remained unprofitable for many years; their

24. GARF, f. R-5446, op. 14a, d. 656, l. 18.
25. GARF, f. R-5446, op. 18a, d. 656, ll. 23, 26.
26. GARF, f. R-5446, op. 23a, d. 105, ll. 40, 42.

debts to the state rose so high that they periodically had to be written off.[27] At the same time the destruction of the most viable peasant farms led to an extremely severe crisis throughout Soviet agriculture. This crisis resulted in the famine of the early 1930s and periodic, smaller outbreaks of famine and serious food problems, which the USSR was unable to escape for decades.

The untimely death of hundreds of thousands of people in the Gulag and the senseless waste in hard labor of energies and talents that could have been of incomparably greater usefulness if they had been at liberty significantly weakened the country's labor capacity.

The special conditions in which the Gulag economy functioned (heightened secrecy and a lack of control) promoted the wide proliferation of padded statistics and false reports. The reminiscences of former prisoners overflow with testimony about how tenaciously and resourcefully people in the camps sought to "pull a *tufta*." "*Tufta* (sometimes: *tukhta*)—scam, deception; chicanery; work done only for appearance; deliberately falsified, inflated indicators in an official report."[28] This term, which came into universal use in the Gulag, reflected an equally universal and daily occurrence in the Gulag, one of the underpinnings of the forced-labor economy. "If it hadn't been for tufta and ammonal, there wouldn't have been a White Sea Canal"; "The Soviet Union rests on *mat* [obscene language], tufta and *blat* [pulling strings]," prisoners used to say.[29] But prisoners were not the only ones who were interested in preserving the system of padded statistics (which often saved their lives); their bosses also had a stake in it.

Many of the high economic indicators of the camp economy were essentially tufta, since they were achieved not through normal organization of production but through predatory exploita-

27. *Spetspereselentsy v Zapadnoi Sibiri. 1930-vesna 1931 g.*, ed. V. P. Danilov and S. A. Krasilnikov (Novosibirsk: EKOR, 1992), p. 12; *Spetspereselentsy v Zapadnoi Sibiri. 1933–1938*, ed. V. P. Danilov and S. A. Krasilnikov (Novosibirsk: EKOR, 1994), pp. 7–8.
28. J. Rossi, *The Gulag Handbook*. The entry *Tufta*.
29. Ibid.

tion of resources. Since they had at their disposal both vast territories for uncontrolled "economic development" and reliable labor resources, the leaders of the NKVD enterprises preferred not to create permanent, long-term projects that required substantial investments, but exploited the most resource-rich areas for brief periods. This was precisely the basis, in particular, of Dalstroi's "economic miracle" in the second half of the 1930s and the nominal "cheapness" of Kolyma gold. This could not go on for long. Whereas the average gold content between 1935 and 1938 (thanks to the exploitation of the richest deposits) was 27 to 19.3 grams per cubic meter of sands washed, in 1946–47 it was already only about 7 grams. Accordingly, the amounts mined dropped sharply as well.

The NKVD economy, which was based on hard physical labor, rejected technical progress. According to 1939 data, mechanized haulage of timber at the People's Commissariat of the Timber Industry, the country's chief timber producer, ran at more than 90 percent, while the figure for the Gulag was about 67 percent.[30] Although in many instances NKVD enterprises were technically equipped much better than similar enterprises of other people's commissariats, they made poorer use of this hardware. Managers at NKVD projects preferred to deal with the chronic problems of the Soviet economy—a shortage of skilled personnel and poor-quality support and repair of mechanisms—by increasing the use of the prisoners' physical capacity. An inspection of Gulag construction projects and the management of NKVD railroad construction in early 1940 showed that a large proportion of the machinery and mechanisms were idle. Excavators were being used at 40 percent of capacity, tractors at 11 percent, and so forth. A powerful imported excavator lay idle at the Volga construction project for three years, and 112 dump trucks at the construction of the Moscow-Minsk highway did not work for more than two months a year.[31]

30. GARF, f. R-5446, op. 24a, d. 2940, l. 2.
31. GARF, f. R-5446, op. 24a, d. 4, ll. 41–42.

As a purveyor of less than outstanding examples of production organization, the Gulag with its "cheap" manpower also had a corrupting effect on the sectors of the economy that were based on civilian labor. Soviet economic people's commissariats, which for objective, systemic reasons had little interest in organizational or technical progress, preferred to deal with many problems by issuing "work assignments" to prisoners. The people's commissariats' pressure on higher party and government bodies with requests for prisoners to be allocated was so heavy that even Stalin could not stand it. At a plenum of the Central Committee of the All-Russian Communist Party (Bolsheviks) in July 1940, he declared:

> You have noticed that the people's commissariats very often ask the NKVD to provide people from the Gulag, from among the criminals. If one takes all our construction projects, I must tell you that one-third of the manpower at the construction projects in the North in the remote corners, in railroad construction, in the forests, one-third of the manpower there are criminal elements. . . . We need to have a reserve rather than take people from the Gulag. This is a disgrace; this is an undesirable practice. The Gulag can be used somewhere in the remote corners, but in the machine-building industry, in the cities, where a criminal is working on the side, and then a noncriminal is working there, I don't know about that, I would say it's very impractical and not altogether proper."[32]

These criticisms by Stalin did not have any serious consequences.

The massive use of prisoners impeded the development of the labor market and the social infrastructure. Prisoner labor became a kind of narcotic for the economy, which it found increasingly difficult to give up by replacing prisoners with civilian workers. The Stalinist system of exploiting prisoner labor was gradually dismantled in the 1950s and 1960s, after Stalin's death.

All these questions—about the actual value of forced labor in

32. RGASPI, f. 71, op. 10, d. 130, ll. 173, 179.

the Soviet industrialization of the 1930s, about the impact of the Gulag economy on the Soviet economic system as a whole, and so on—need further study. The problem of the Gulag's "intellectual zone," which this chapter did not address, requires special attention. So far there is little known material about the use of the labor of arrested engineers and scientists in special units of the OGPU-NKVD during the 1930s—which makes it all the more important to continue searching for it.

If one compares the enormous volume of archival information about the economic activity of the Gulag with the extent to which the information is utilized, it is clear that research on this topic has only begun. Documents from the central archives have not been put to significant use. There are even fewer works on the Gulag's individual economic units, based on local material. But if the initial attempts at such studies have not yet met with much success, the fact that such efforts are at least being made inspires some optimism.

7 ECONOMIC CRIME AND PUNISHMENT

Eugenia Belova

This chapter analyzes the efforts of Soviet authorities to deter and prosecute "illegal" economic activities in the 1930s through the party's top control commission. Major economic positions were filled by the Politburo itself, where appointments dominated its agenda. Party members were supposed to be a new type of *homo soveticus*, dedicated to building socialism. According to official Soviet descriptions of the planned economy, all exchanges were planned, managers were loyal, and everyone was motivated by the goal of building socialism. There was no room for economic crimes and misdemeanors. We show, to the contrary, that economic agents, most of them party members, regularly broke the rules of the leadership, in spite of the real threat of punishment. Why would a planned economy managed by party members be so prone to violations of economic rules and laws?

The opening of the Soviet state and party archives provides an opportunity to study the "unofficial" behavior of the managers of the economy's resources; namely, factory managers, industrial ministry officials, and regional authorities. Such "managers of production" (*khoziaistvenniki*) were judged by concrete economic results—production, adherence to labor plans, fulfillment of pro-

The author is grateful to the Hoover Institution for its support of this project.

duction assortments, cost reduction plans, and the like. Their goal was to fulfill their plans, using any means at their disposal, even if that meant violating rules and laws. The pioneering work of Joseph Berliner (1957) provided the first conclusive insights into the real life of Soviet managers. Using interviews with former Soviet managers to pierce the veil of official secrecy, Berliner found routine falsification, the use of unofficial resources, and the trading of resources by enterprise "pushers" *(tolkachi)*—all of which violated Soviet law.[1]

The Soviet system used, among other organizations, centralized control commissions to detect and punish party-member managers. This chapter draws primarily upon the formerly secret archives of the Party Control Commission (KPK) in the period 1934–1939 located in the archives of the Hoover Institution.[2] KPK had the extraordinary right to interrogate officials of rank up to minister and of all branches of industry and administration including the secret police (OGPU). Regular law enforcement agencies such as the courts or militia had narrower ranges of operation. Accordingly, KPK files provide extraordinary insights into the illicit economic behavior even at high levels.

THE SOVIET LEGAL SYSTEM

The logic of the Soviet administrative-command system (described in the chapters by Rees, Davies, and Gregory) was for the party to set general objectives and intervene in specific cases, while Gosplan and other functional committees set targets for industrial ministries and regional authorities. A whole range of agencies monitored plan fulfillment ranging from the party itself, to military inspectors, and to Gosplan. Yet in spite of the multi-

1. Joseph Berliner, *Factory and Manager in the USSR* (Cambridge, Mass.: Harvard University Press, 1957).
2. Hoover Institution for War, Revolution and Peace, and Rosarkhiv, Documents of the Communist Party and the Soviet State. Party Control Commission. Originals are held in RGANI (former archive of the Central Committee of the Communist Party of the Soviet Union), Moscow.

tude of controls, substantial discretion by managers of production could not be avoided; actual transactions among sellers and buyers, other than for a few key commodities, could not be planned from the center. Industrial ministries and their administrations managed most of the operational planning and resource distributions. The temptation was strong for managers to deal directly with one another out of sight of planners.

In market economies, constitutions, commercial laws, customs, and other generally accepted practices define the legal rules of the game. Although the Soviet Union of the 1930s had formal civil and criminal laws, codified laws played little role, and court independence was limited. Each Soviet republic had its own criminal code, many adopted before the creation of the Union of Soviet Socialist Republics in 1924, but the criminal justice system was mainly directed from Moscow. Throughout the 1920s and 1930s, criminal laws were frequently updated and modified by government and party decrees, and the number of activities designated as economic crimes expanded.[3]

The criminalization of economic offenses was a logical consequence of state ownership. Economic plans approved by the state and party were *the law*; therefore, failure to fulfill plans represented a violation of basic law. Managers of production had to "fulfill their plans" or else be branded as criminals. However, plan obligations were multidimensional, calling for fulfilling production targets, cost reductions, capital investment plans, delivery plans, and the like. Activities that took place outside the formal planning system were automatic violations of the law; there was virtually no room for free business activities. The "plan-law" changed every quarter or even more frequently when party officials intervened. With multidimensional planning, it was not clear

3. For example, on November 23, 1929, the government declared low-quality production a criminal offense, punishable by a minimum (!) of five years of imprisonment; *Sobranie Zakonov SSSR*, no. 2, 1930. In 1934, the government made cheating of customers in retail stores an offense punishable by a maximum of ten years of imprisonment; *Sobranie Zakonov SSSR*, no. 4, 1934.

who had failed to meet their plan obligations. Production managers, confronted with delivery failures, construction delays, and worker shortages, had to decide what plans to fulfill. When they appealed to higher authorities, they were usually told to make do with less. The Soviet archives brim with petitions, pleas, threats, complaints, and claims, designed to prove that any plan failure was someone else's fault. In this confusing environment, the dividing line between doing what was right to fulfill the plan and operating for personal gain was blurred. Both honest and dishonest managers had to go outside the formal planning system, but the honest manager did so for the benefit of the enterprise, the dishonest manager to line his pockets. Under Soviet law, both have potentially committed crimes.

CONTROL COMMISSIONS

The framers of the Soviet system separated planning from enforcement and punishment. Although the top leadership meted out high-level punishment at times, more routine investigations and punishments were the purview of the courts and control commissions, the latter headed by top party leaders. The Bolsheviks inherited their first control agency from the tsarist government, which became in May 1918 the People's Commissariat of State Control. From 1923 to 1934, the major control commission was the People's Commissariat of Worker-Peasant Inspection, the much-feared Rabkrin (TsKK-NKRKI).[4] The XVII Party Congress in 1934 split Rabkrin into two new commissions: the State Commission of Soviet Control (KSK), and the Commission of Party Control (KPK), which reported directly to the Central Party Com-

4. The organization was at the same time the Communist Party Central Committee Control Department (TsKK) and the People's Commissariat of Workers' and Peasants' Inspection, or NKRKI. On this subject, see more in E.A. Rees, *State Control in Soviet Russia: The Rise and Fall of the Workers' and Peasants' Inspectorate, 1920–1934* (London: Macmillan, 1987), and J. Arch Getty, *The Origins of the Great Purges: The Soviet Communist Party Reconsidered, 1933–1938* (Cambridge: Cambridge University Press, 1985).

mittee and was vested with the power to discipline party members. The secretary of the Central Committee of the party, L. M. Kaganovich, was appointed the first chairman of KPK. N. I. Ezhov, who later became the main operator of the Great Terror, became the deputy chairman; the two secretaries of KPK's Collegium were M. F. Shkiriatov and E. Yaroslavsky.[5]

The main objectives of KPK were to ensure fulfillment of party-state decrees and to protect the "purity" and discipline of party ranks. In contrast to the state control commission, KPK plenipotentiaries were independent of regional party leaders, providing the central party apparatus with an avenue for investigating the powerful local party organizations, and KPK also included industrial groups (usually composed of two or three members) and regional plenipotentiaries (each assisted by several dozen of staff). Staff members were recruited from the best workers of the former regional Rabkrin committees.[6] Selected members of local party collegiums, approved by Kaganovich and Ezhov, were to serve KPK.[7]

Throughout the 1930s, for a number of reasons, KPK became increasingly involved in economic wrongdoing cases. First, most managers were party members and had to be disciplined by the party itself. Under the party slogan "Cadres are all important," economic problems became personnel matters and vice versa. Only the party had the right to punish its own members. In cases where a party member was convicted in a court proceeding, party expulsion followed almost automatically, but the initiative of turning the case over to the courts was left to the discretion of party control commissions. Party membership brought with it advantages and privileges that could be abused. As Shkiriatov ex-

5. The leaders of the new commissions, both KPK and KSK, were the former members of TsKK-NKRKI.

6. Industrial groups corresponded to industrial ministries: the Ministry of Heavy Industry, Light Industry, Railroad Transport, Timber Industry, etc. Additional administrative KPK groups were also created: the group of local government, finance, housing and municipal services, etc.

7. RGANI, f. 6, op. 1, d. 23, l. 22.

pressed it in 1936: "Having a party card (*partbilet*) provides admission everywhere and anytime. He can enter any office—he is a communist, they'll let him in anywhere. Where a non-party official cannot go, he can. "[8] The economic value of partbilets can be seen in an active market in the sale of such uncovered by various KPK investigations. A Kazakhstan KPK commissioner declared in a 1934 meeting: "In this party organization, somewhere in the neighborhood of 20,000 partbilets have been lost. We have a huge number of facts about trade in and sale of partbilets, and . . . the loss of partbilets, actually not loss but speculation in partbilets."[9]

Second, KPK had to monitor the interactions of managers of production. If their careers were to flourish and if they were to avoid punishment, party-member managers had to produce results, even if they had to act against higher interests. As industrial managers, party members could grant or withhold favors. As regional leaders, they controlled local materials, scarce housing, and vacation privileges. As controllers of resources, they had something to offer other controllers of resources, creating a fertile ground for deals and exchanges. Moreover, party members from the same locality found their fates interwoven. A local party boss's record would be soiled if local enterprises (also run by party members) failed to meet their plans. Accordingly, regional and industrial elite formed tight-knit cliques, united by common bonds.[10] Those who made troubles for the clique were removed from their posts, thereby losing all the attendant privileges. The presumed independence of KPK from local party organizations made it the sole agency capable of breaking these cliques.

Third, in the absence of market discipline and bankruptcy, there were no automatic penalties for mismanagement; KPK had to take "poor" enterprise managers to task for uneconomical use

8. Ibid., d. 15, l. 37.
9. Ibid., d. 7, l. 62.
10. On this subject see more in James R. Harris, "The Purging of Local Cliques in the Urals Region," in Sheila Fitzpatrick, ed., *Stalinism: New Directions* (London: Routledge, 1999), pp. 262–85); James R. Harris, *The Great Urals: Regionalism and the Evolution of the Soviet System* (Ithaca, N.Y.: Cornell University Press, 1999).

of resources and for cheating others. In a market economy, courts arbitrate legal disputes and bring violators of economic laws to justice. Soviet legal codes made many offenses that would normally be considered civil violations into criminal offenses. Soviet courts were not the main means of enforcing economic laws. A court system can function effectively only if plaintiffs are prepared to bring their claims for adjudication. Unplanned product exchange or low-quality goods—crimes against the Soviet state and against its main law, the plan—were typically "victimless" crimes; they represented voluntary exchanges in which both parties intended to continue their dealings. When no party to a "crime" is prepared to complain, the state needs an agent as its advocate to uncover economic crimes. Control commissions, with great access to information at any level in the management chain, could detect a broader range of illegal economic activities than could a conventional justice system that relies on signals from disgruntled parties.[11]

Neither the militia nor procurator offices were considered fully reliable, and they were placed under scrutiny by KPK officials. KPK plenipotentiaries from different regions in the third meeting of KPK in 1936 complained of the lack of responsibility and qualification of judges and court members and of excessive red tape, and even of theft of court-case documents: "When we examined the disappearance of files from Bukhara party committee, we found out that files also had been disappearing from the procurator's office—a total of 16 cases. In the whole, we found no criminal investigation offices where they had no disappearance of documents."[12] A 1934 report of the transportation group of

11. Disputes between enterprises were handled by a special institution, Arbitration Courts, which had less importance than control commissions; their decisions could be overruled by ministries or local administrative bodies. Arbitration procedure was also determined by plan-law. There was no real contract law; rather, the government would issue each year general directives for contracting, which were supposed to be implemented by actual contracting parties in the course of what was called the "contracting campaign."

12. RGANI, f. 6, op. 1, d. 13, l. 134.

KPK cites the case of the Poltava transportation procurator, who brought to the court only six cases of theft on the railroads of fifty-three investigated, stating, "The transportation procurator office does not care a lot about theft and embezzlement."[13] Courts were also criticized for not prosecuting, or even collaborating with private mediators, who assisted enterprise clients in making the railroads pay for the damage and loss of shipped goods.[14] Judges often received reprimands,[15] were expelled from the party, or fired. A KPK plenipotentiary from Uzbekistan reported that the Uzbek party control commission expelled twenty-two district procurators, nine investigators, thirteen judges, and two members of the republican supreme court; the KPK official himself fired three more judges, seven investigators, two members of courts, two regional, and three district procurators.[16] In Kuibyshev region, KPK fired seventy of the total of 120 judges.[17] Also, KPK uncovered a number of cases of "violations of revolutionary legality and overreaching of authority" by the militia, involving misuse of funds and possible embezzlement.[18]

An influential KPK official, Yaroslavsky, worried about the fine line between party disciplinary punishment and court sentences in a KPK meeting in 1936: "Sometimes [KPK] substitutes for Soviet courts. Sometimes [KPK] committees discuss every misdeed by an official, and they feel themselves obliged to levy disciplinary punishments. We must rigorously distinguish between the cases that should be considered as offenses against party and those against state."[19] In their investigations, KPK staff never referenced what paragraph of the legal code had been violated; if they referred to any "laws" at all, it was to ad hoc party-state decrees, although even those decrees were not necessary justifica-

13. Ibid., d. 36, ll. 62–74.
14. Ibid., d. 37, ll. 22–40.
15. Ibid., d. 40, l. 122.
16. Ibid., d. 13, l. 150.
17. Ibid., d. 14 , ll. 138–47.
18. Ibid., d. 38, ll. 152–43.
19. Ibid., d. 15, ll. 88–115.

tions for their cases. More often cases were initiated and treated at the discretion of KPK officials, who had an imprecise understanding of what was legal and illegal.

THE HONEST MANAGER'S DILEMMA

In the Soviet system, even honest and loyal agents could not achieve their goals by obeying rules. To understand the honest manager's dilemma, consider a typical factory director. His factory is part of the industrial ministry system: It receives raw materials from the centralized sources and produces inputs for the other participants of the industrial network. Our manager is seeking only the benefits that accrue legally from plan fulfillment (bonuses, perks, advancement) and is not interested in self-enrichment at the expense of the enterprises. Such a manager could not avoid engaging in "criminal" activities, in spite of the best of intentions.

The manager's first problem is that he can legally obtain the materials needed to meet his targets only through unreliable official supply channels. Either he has been allotted too little or he has been allotted enough by the ministry but the supplies fail to come. Confronted with deficits of raw materials, his "legal" remedy is to complain to his superiors. He bombards his superiors in the ministry and local party officials with requests for assistance, but the answer is: "Make do with less; find internal reserves." The market-economy solution—buy more inputs—is illegal, even if he has the money. Factory funds are limited to use for strictly designated purposes. Our manager can either accept plan failure or try to obtain additional resources through "illegal channels." Our manager dispatches his expediters (*tolkachi*) to his suppliers, to persuade them to deliver both the planned amounts of materials (which is by no means certain) and supplies in excess of those planned. Good tolkachi are costly; our manager has to pay their salaries, travel expenses, and living expenses, and give them incentives to outcompete the tolkachi of dozens of other desperate en-

terprises. His staffing plan, which is subject to strict governmental
control, does not list supply agents. So, our manager has to ma-
nipulate his factory's budget in order to pay tolkachi. In addition
to violating payroll rules, our manager's use of the tolkach em-
broils him in yet another criminal activity: Tolkachi undermine
"plan discipline," that is, governmental control over resource distribution, and are outlawed. The tolkach's job is therefore risky,
and our manager must offer him a generous contract.[20]

The competition for supplies puts our manager's suppliers in
a position to earn extra profits. His suppliers could: (1) ask for a
price above the planned price, (2) offer inferior quality materials,
or (3) agree to deliver materials in exchange for products from
our manager's factory. For our manager (1) and (2) are not crimes
per se, but they constitute the crime of speculation for the supplier. The third is a serious crime for both: illegal product exchange. Now, in addition to the main problem of plan fulfillment,
our manager has to worry about the consequences of his illegal
activities, which may be hard to conceal. If he has to pay more
than was planned, his factory's budget has a "hole," which audi-
tors can label a waste of financial resources, mismanagement, or
even embezzlement. To cover these unplanned expenses, our manager may have to apply for additional "turnover funds" from the
local branch of the state bank. He will probably be told by his
bank to do without. If he is successful in obtaining the additional
credits, he exposes himself to the jeopardy of an avoidable audit.

Confronted with the need to pay more for his inputs, our manager can obtain unplanned revenues by charging his customers
"speculative" prices above the planned price, just as his supplier
has done to him. He is officially allowed to sell some small portion

20. For example, the chairman of the Rostov supply agency (Ukrainian branch
of the Heavy Industry) proposed the following contract to his tolkachi: fixed salary
(400 rubles); extra 6 rubles for the shipping/loading of each planned (*po nariadam*)
carload of metal if it was above 80 percent of planned amount; an extra 12 rubles
for each additional load of low-quality metal (which was also a valuable input);
living expenses of an agent are equal to the day-wage paid at the official work place.
RGANI, f. 6, op. 1, d. 40, ll. 108–17.

(usually 5 percent) of output at higher-than-planned prices if he exceeds his production target.[21] Given the long line of consumers, our manager can accept the highest offer, which may exceed the official price by several hundred percent. Our manager can also deliver to customers who pay immediately rather than to the planned ones who delay payments.[22] Although it was officially allowed to sell above-plan output at higher prices, it is unclear whether our manager might be accused of speculation if the profit margin is too high.

Suppose that, despite sales at above-plan prices, our manager still does not have enough revenue to buy his needed deficit inputs. To this point, he can only be accused of speculation—that is, of selling at too-high prices; he has not sold any planned output to undesignated customers.[23] To gain enough revenue to buy his inputs, he decides to sell deficit production without authorization—a crime of illegal product exchange because it takes place entirely outside the planning system.

Our honest manager's problems are not over, although he, by this point, has broken the "plan-law" more than five times. He still needs extra cash to provide incentives for his workers, his tolkachi and for "presents" to local party-state officials, and perhaps for his higher-ups in the ministry to make sure they are on his side in case of trouble. Given the strict controls over his bank accounts, he has two ways to raise this extra cash. He can submit false invoices to the state bank; or he could resubmit bills that

21. In reality, the share of relatively free marketed output was determined by the probability of detection, which varies greatly between industries.

22. For example, directors of furniture factories of Forest Industry had to deliver the majority of the products to the central trading agency. The agency, however, was slow to pay and the factory chose to sell furniture to respectable customers who paid immediately, mostly governmental organizations. RGANI, f. 6, op. 1, d. 27, ll. 87–95.

23. In fact, KPK investigators found that many branches were selling large percentages of their output through this mechanism "without orders" (*bez naryadov*). For example, a Kiev factory sold almost 18 percent of its turnover. Even high-priority coal mines in the Donbass region were able to sell 15 percent of their output without orders. RGANI, f. 6, op. 1, d. 23, l. 272; ibid., d. 34, l. 101.

were paid earlier, and hope that the bank would not notice. Another option is offered by a government decree, permitting the free sale of consumer goods products produced from defective materials through "utilization shops." In fact, he has a small shop, and he buys some "defective" inputs that have fallen outside the planning system and sells finished products in utilization shops. The manager even classifies normal materials as defective to take advantage of this loophole.

What are our manager's chances of being caught, and if he is caught, what punishments will he face? What steps can he take to reduce his vulnerability to criminal charges? He must choose a course of action that minimizes the risk of being punished and brings the maximum gain. An adroit manager would be able to judge which "crimes" are more risky than others. The skilled manager would also know approaches that could be taken to reduce the risks of detection and of punishment.

KPK'S ADMINISTRATION OF JUSTICE

KPK had an arsenal of "punitive" (*karatelny*) powers, which it could apply to party members. The most lenient punishment was to "place on notice" (*postavit na vid*). More serious punishments were to issue a reprimand (*vygovor*), or a stern reprimand (*strogy vygovor*). These reprimands would be placed in the member's party book and would remain on his permanent record unless removed by action of some responsible authority. In some cases, the reprimand would be accompanied by the ban on holding responsible positions for a period of time. The most severe punishment was removal from the party. Or KPK investigators could turn matters over to the prosecutor, and the courts could then sentence party members to jail or even impose the death sentence.

The officials of KPK can be divided into those who insisted on the strict adherence to the law calling for the most severe punishment and those who were prepared to excuse illegal actions depending on their rationale. The latter employed a sort of psychological analysis to reveal the true reason for illegal actions. Discussions in KPK meetings provide striking evidence of the fuzziness and variations of the controllers' understanding of what was wrong and right, as well as of the imprecision of the dividing line between theft and pragmatic dealings.[24] The KPK officials had to rely upon their subjective understanding of "honesty," which was not uniform, either. A KPK delegate from Kursk, Chubin, took a pragmatic view of honesty concerning opportunities for stealing of grain from warehouses:

> *Chubin*: Our inspectors—honest people (laughter in the hall)—together with the grain procurement agency officer decided to check on the warehouses, at night. They approached one storehouse, it was open. They took one sack of grain and took it away. They entered another warehouse, took another sack and took it away. They took a sack from the third one, and nobody even noticed.
> *A retort from the hall*: And are they honest people? (Laughter in the hall)
> *Chubin*: Yes, they are, because grain is preserved there in such a way that every honest man can take it. (Laughter in the hall).[25]

Stalingrad KPK plenipotentiary Frenkel surprised the same meeting by saying that there were certain cases when appropriation of products could not be considered as a theft and that there were "some authorities in Moscow" who supported this view.[26] The hard-line chairman of KPK, Kaganovich, demanded their names, retorting that there should be no doubts that when workers steal parts it is common theft. Frenkel defended his pragmatist view with the story that he was told by a state farm director. They were usually assigned construction plans without materials being

24. J. Arch Getty, "Pragmatists and Puritans: The Rise and Fall of the Party Control Commission," working paper, CREES, University of Pittsburgh, no. 1208, 1997.

25. RGANI, f. 6, op. 1, d. 13, l. 211.

26. Getty, "Pragmatists and Puritans," discusses this case referring to the archival materials of TsKhSD. RGANI, f. 6, op. 1, d. 5, ll. 5–56.

provided to implement them. The dilemma the managers faced was whether to follow the official path and wait in vain for the supplies and finally fail to complete the task, or to break the law and follow the advice of supply agents to get glass and nails in exchange for meat and bread. Frenkel insisted that the true criminals were the supply agents rather than the farm directors, whereas according to the Soviet law enforcement paradigm, which did not account explicitly for planning errors, the managers were to be held responsible.

The conflict between pragmatic and hard-line views, each extreme of which was criticized by the party and KPK leaders, caused a downward shift of punishment outcomes. Controllers who belonged to the hard-line camp were criticized for overreaction, and the Bureau of KPK, in their final resolutions, applied less strict penalties. However, when "pragmatic" KPK controllers proposed relatively mild punishments, the Bureau of KPK rarely imposed harsher punishments.

Analysis of the large number of criminal cases of managerial abuse handled by KPK during the 1930s bears evidence to the fact that there was no uniform standard of punishment, although KPK officials agreed that standards should be uniform. Internal KPK discussions show that a particular plenipotentiary's style and quality of work depended on his work environment; plenipotentiaries were known to change their style when transferred.[27] Yet KPK leaders asserted that it was extremely important to strive for the exact implementation of the decrees regardless of the individual temperament of controllers.[28] Uniformity of punishment was hard to achieve not only because of different philosophies within KPK. The main task of KPK was the proper execution of certain party-state decrees rather than punishment of particular offenses, but the decrees hardly ever specified what kind of punishment should be applied for their breach. Moreover, KPK work was

27. RGANI, f. 6, op. 1, d. 14, ll. 79–86.
28. RGANI, f. 6, op. 1, d. 14, ll. 148–17.

often organized as campaigns; immediately after a decree was issued, KPK engaged in hectic activity pursuing its implementation.
This effort decayed over time as controllers were given newer assignments.[29] Different punishments for the same offense could be
related purely to timing.

TYPES OF OFFENSES

Files of KPK for this period cover more than three thousand cases
of investigations of economic officials. Although there is no simple way to classify these cases, we can single out the most typical
types of crimes and misdemeanors: falsification, quality distortion, illegal product exchange, speculation, embezzlement, and
bribery.

Falsification and Quality Distortion

Managers were investigated for providing false information
about their enterprises, primarily to planning authorities. The
most common offense was for a manager to understate his capacity to receive easier production targets. When such falsifications
were unmasked, punishment was usually not severe. For example,
the director of Mozherez metal works, as well as his supervisors in
the trust and Gosplan, got reprimands for setting an "artificially
reduced production program" and for failing to use the full capacity of the equipment of the principal factory's shop.[30] The director
of the Karl Libkhnekht factory was only placed on notice for re-

---

29. For example, on December 30, 1934, a decree prohibiting any increase of
the salaries was issued. The campaign started in January when KPK plenipotentiaries
disclosed a number of cases of neglecting the order. They generously gave reprimands and warnings to the managers (RGANI, f. 6, op. 1, d. 41; RGANI, f. 6, op.
1, d. 42). By the spring this campaign was over and the salary issue was dropped
from the agenda. Besides, the number of controllers was not sufficient to provide
uniform coverage of all fields of economic activities as well as geography. The minutes of the Bureau of KPK (RGANI, f. 6, op. 1) contain numerous campaigns of
KPK controllers on their work under permanent stress. They asked for extra persons
to be sent into their region or to be added to a group controlling some industry.

30. RGANI, f. 6, op. 1, d. 23, ll. 50–55.

ducing reported productive capacity by more than half, which
meant that his factory easily overfulfilled the plan even though it
was operating with spare capacity: "He was anyway able to give
307 tons, that is, 50 percent more than was planned," the KPK
report reads in justifying the light sentence.[31] Although easy plans
made the manager's job more secure, negotiations with planning
organizations for reduced targets took a long time. Everyday
problems demanded immediate actions. Moreover, managers
could fail in this "disinformation game."

Falsification of financial reports and invoices was a more
straightforward remedy than target reductions. Managers submitted false and/or duplicate invoices, made forged calculations for
construction projects, and engaged in other financial misreporting
to receive more cash. The files show that such practices were
widespread and that it often took authorities considerable time to
detect them. If some pattern of falsification brought positive results and was not uncovered immediately, managers would use it
systematically. For example, managers of the Sprinkler Trust,
which produced fire extinguishers, submitted invoices for incomplete tasks to the State Bank with impunity and received cash and
credits for duplicate bills. The head of the trust and his deputy
succeeded in collecting substantial amounts of cash: In April 1934
alone, they submitted seventy-five faulty documents and got
712,000 rubles. After KPK's investigation, it was resolved to dismiss both managers and reconsider their party status conditional
on the court verdict. In addition, KPK decided to publicize this
case in the press.[32] Another KPK investigation of several heavy
industry plants showed that it was possible to use faulty calculations systematically because banks were not able to uncover de-
ceptions for six to nine months.[33] The directors of the heavy
industry plants received party reprimands but remained in their
positions: KPK concluded that these directors did not check per-

31. Ibid., d. 34, ll. 168–72.
32. Ibid., d. 34, ll. 190–95.
33. Ibid., d. 40, ll. 179–82.

sonally on the documents and, trusting their subordinates, signed false invoices. In other words, the blame was shifted to subordinates.

A government decree of March 4, 1933, "On the order of sales of consumer goods produced by utilization shops," legalized the use of defective resources as inputs for special shops producing consumer goods. Such production could be sold outside the centralized distribution network; enterprises could market it freely and keep the profits. Producers learned that virtually any material could be declared defective and the reported quality of output decreased. A KPK survey of the wool works in the light industry ministry showed that reported average quality dropped by three times only in four months of late 1933 to early 1934.[34] "Utilization shops" accepted defective items which they easily fixed and then sold as high-quality goods produced in excess of plan.[35] Kuntsevsky works stimulated low-quality production of sewing-machine parts, since it was such a profitable business: In the first quarter of 1934 alone, some thirty state enterprises not eligible to purchase Kuntsevsky's output were served by its "utilization shop."[36] Stalingradsky Tractor Works assembled and marketed tractors using parts marked as defective. Although the manager was warned that further illegal marketing would lead to severe punishment, KPK plenipotentiaries concluded: "It is certainly expedient to continue assembly of tractors from defective parts because it allows production of an extra 600 machines per year. . . . Those tractors could be used under less strained conditions."[37] Again, KPK's remedy was to include such unplanned production in the centralized supply system: Although production of low-quality machines did not have to be reported in planned output, the distribution of these machines was proposed to be done in a planned manner. Similarly, KPK ordered cancellation of the selling by Yaroslavsky tire works of restored tires to un-

34. Ibid., d. 24, l. 89.
35. Ibid., d. 36, ll. 136–40.
36. Ibid., d. 30, ll. 48–52.
37. Ibid., d. 27, ll. 69–73.

planned consumers and placed such tires into Yaroslavsky's general allocation plan, giving some preferences to those consumers who fulfill rubber recycling plans.[38]

Illegal Product Exchange

Illegal product exchange, that is, trading of materials among factories outside normal planned distribution channels, was one of the most frequent economic crimes of the 1930s. Consider the following cases: In 1933–34, Dzerzhinsky works exchanged its product—window glass—for dairy products and fish to supply the workers' canteen.[39] The director of Dzerzhinsky works was brought before the court and expelled from the party. Additionally, the head of the supervising trust and the deputy of the ministry of light industry received stern reprimands because they did not actively fight against such illegal transactions. Coal mines of the Kadievugol trust in Donbass struck deals with a chemical factory to sell twenty carloads of coal in exchange for the sales of eight carloads of roofing felt; two cooperatives were supplied with about ninety tons of coal in exchange for overalls.[40] The Bureau of KPK turned this case over to the Procurator General with a recommendation to prosecute the persons involved.

The above-mentioned case of Yaroslavsky tire works demonstrates the breadth of enterprise connection networks. Requests from "preferred customers" were accepted even for products that were not produced normally: "An order for 10 Buick tires from the administration of the Ivanovo Regional Party committee was found. The factory does not produce tires of this size. However, the management accepted it. A number of organizations were supplied in the manner of direct product exchange."[41] The managers of Yaroslavsky tire works avoided severe punishment, however,

38. Ibid., d. 32, ll. 137–41.
39. Ibid., d. 23, l. 27.
40. Ibid., ll. 39–48.
41. Ibid., d. 32, ll. 137–41.

because KPK investigators found that the planned targets were met. The director was excused because he had just recently been appointed and his deputies escaped with reprimands. But one of the partners of Yaroslavsky works—Moscow bread trust, which supplied confectionery to the factory's groceries in exchange for the tires—attracted special attention of KPK. All the managers of this trust got reprimands.

Direct product exchange sometimes took on quite sophisticated forms: Managers price-discriminated among consumers according to their ability to supply what the factory needed. Governmental and industrial consumers who could provide needed exchange goods got products at low fixed prices while other consumers bought at higher prices. A sugar factory in Georgia supplied unplanned industrial consumers, who had valuable goods to exchange, at 10 kopecks per ton, while the "population" had to buy it for 10 rubles per ton—100 times higher.[42] The whole sugar factory management was removed from their jobs and a criminal process was initiated.

We cannot tell from KPK records the share of pure barter in illegal product exchange versus the share of monetary transactions between reciprocal "preferred customers." KPK controllers used "direct product exchange" to denote both "barter" and preferred-customer financial transactions. For KPK controllers, as well as for the enterprises, the monetary component of the transaction was unimportant if low nominal prices were used. Only the fact of unplanned reallocation of resources mattered. Barter was the most inspection-proof method of exchange since it left no traces in accounting records and checking the real physical state of inventories required too much effort.

Speculation

In cases of unplanned production, where the price was not set officially, unusually high profit margins could lead to the accusa-

42. Ibid., d. 36, ll. 141–45.

tion of speculation. The honest manager's dilemma indicated that managers dealt with two different economic paradigms: plan and market. Some inputs were received at fixed prices through official but unreliable channels, while other inputs were bought at higher prices through unplanned transactions. The official prices of producers' goods were based on costs; they did not take demand into account and included high rates of turnover tax. Latent price increases spread across the economy, since partners to transactions were state enterprises. A high degree of specialization, characteristic of the Soviet economy, prevented market-type competition. Nothing, except perhaps severe police controls, could prevent producers from marking up planned prices. Price markups could be interpreted as the crime of speculation. The KPK files reveal that there was enormous variation in the penalties for this sort of crime.

Consider two typical "speculation" cases: Dzerzhinsky works of the light industry ministry sold window glass for 200–250 rubles instead of the official price of 48 rubles.[43] Kuntsevsky tire works's utilization shop bought low-quality semifinished inputs for "0,3 kopeck per kg and sold the final goods at the prices exceeding costs by 300%."[44] KPK turned the first case over to the Procurator's office (as well as the cases of many directors of glass and porcelain enterprises who stepped over the 5 percent threshold for free market sales). In the second case, the director got away with a party reprimand and remained at the same position.

Embezzlement and Bribery

The manager's success in avoiding punishment depended on his connections inside the factory as well as outside. The manager had to be confident that his staff was reliable, since there had

43. Ibid., d. 23, l. 27.
44. Ibid., d. 30, ll. 48–52. Noteworthy, this controller did not provide precise data on sales prices. It looks as if he was just fascinated by the scale of numbers: inconceivable share of kopeck vs. no less fabulous 300 percent.

to be collaboration among the factory's bookkeeper, commercial director, and shop stewards. The manager also had to be able to rely on the support and protection of local party and state authorities, and he had to have good relations with his superiors in the ministry, who might need to look the other way at times. The maintenance of internal and external connections required an incentive system, which could produce loyalty at any level. The manager's "loyalty network" was to some extent automatic, not requiring material incentives ("bribes"). Local party officials wanted to show good performance from their local enterprises, and ministry officials, too, wanted good performance from the enterprises under their supervision. But cover for enterprises engaging in illegal activities could be risky for participants in the manager's loyalty circle. If transgressions were uncovered by an independent authority, such as KPK, external members of the circle could themselves be punished. The benefits for high-ranking officials were provided by the party according to their position in the hierarchy, and these benefits were supposed to be high enough to prevent bribery and self-providing.

In the May 1934 session of the Bureau of KPK, KPK plenipotentiaries presented the case of the East Siberian agency for procurement of exportable furs, Zagotpushnina: "Over a number of years, the disgusting tradition of impudent self-providing and bribery of chief local and party authorities developed." Key members of the regional elite received gifts in the form of food, commodities, expensive hunting rifles, and valuable furs from a special "incentive fund" that was intended to provide rewards for hunters.[45] The director of Zagotpushnina was removed to a lower position, the chairman of the local state office was dismissed, brought before the court, and expelled from the party; other responsible members of staff were punished and arrested. Investigations of Zagotpushnina branches in other regions—Urals, West Siberia, and Kazakhstan—made it apparent that corruption and

45. Ibid., d. 29, ll. 48–82; ibid., d. 38, l. 160.

bribery were not limited to East Siberia. An inspection conducted in 1933 in 27 regional branches of Zagotpushnina resulted in 151 subordinate employees being brought before the court; of these, four were shot. In this case, too, all levels of the loyalty network were punished: from the local party leaders who accepted gifts and bribes to the low-level managers who carried out embezzlements.

Illegal transactions were possible because the whole production unit and its supervisors were involved. Investigations by KPK uncovered many cases of collaboration by heads of trusts, branch administrations, and even ministries, who did not deter their subordinates from illegal activities. On the contrary, enterprise superiors fought for the lower planned targets and low norms of production quality, and they allowed trusts and enterprises to have special "reserve funds" to serve consumers who applied directly to them. Customers in illegal transactions sometimes even included local administrative and party bodies. A KPK report on the illegal product exchange undertaken by the Yaroslavsky tire works reported: "The array of unplanned customers includes local organizations from enterprises to the city party committee and secret police (OGPU) commandant's office."[46] A Rostov supply agency bookkeeper explained to a KPK official why he acceded to illegal product exchange: "I know that it was formally a violation of law, but, as long as the state organizations were served, I did not see any damage to the state and therefore did not inform controllers; moreover, in some cases allocations were made on personal orders of the director." In this case KPK plenipotentiaries considered this justification an example of bureaucratic behavior: Even if the bureaucrat is completely aware of the illegality of a transaction, he will not report it if it is approved by superiors.[47] The case of the Rostov supply agency prompted the punishment of those who were considered responsible at all levels:

46. Ibid., d. 32, ll. 137–41.
47. Ibid., d. 40, ll. 108–17.

The authorities in the ministry and in the local party body received stern reprimands; the deputy director of the Rostov supply agency was dismissed with stern reprimand (although plenipotentiary proposed to expel him from the party); a criminal investigation by Russian Federation procurator was initiated, and KPK also raised the question of dissolving the corrupt Rostov supply agency.

PUNISHMENT REVERSAL AND REHABILITATION

Paradoxically, side by side with broad repression campaigns, KPK rules of punishment introduced patterns of rehabilitation and even impunity for the managers of production as well as for the party-state authorities punished for economic crimes. The most common form of KPK punishment was the party reprimand, which could be a standard reprimand or a severe reprimand. These reprimands were placed in the party member's record, but they could be removed from the record if a manager was able to prove loyalty and collect good references from his party-state supervisors. A KPK official, Bekker, supported the practice of removing reprimands from records in the Third Assembly of KPK in 1936: "If a person corrects himself, we remove the reprimand. It is this that makes an advantage of party control: it removes reprimands after 3–4 inspections."[48] However, Bekker's opinion was not supported by other KPK members, who argued that the party reprimand had lost its power and could not serve as an effective tool of enforcement. Deputy chairman of KPK, Shkiriatov, illustrated his concern with too frequent use of reprimands. He cited the case of a collective farm director who had received eighteen reprimands since becoming a candidate for party membership; Shkiriatov conjectured that this manager had grown accustomed to this penalty and simply expected a new reprimand when his next failure occurred.[49] A number of speakers presented

48. Ibid., d. 13, ll. 109–54.
49. Ibid., d. 15.

similar evidence: Some communists had more than ten reprimands. The KPK secretary, Yaroslavsky, noted sarcastically to rising laughter in the hall: "Sometimes two to four pages are needed
to be pasted to a member's card to provide space for recording all
punishments."[50] Not only were reprimands becoming accepted as
routine; they were routinely reversed, especially for the heads of
trusts and enterprises. The chairman of KPK, Ezhov, complained
that reprimanded directors were readily excused by local party
organizations.[51]

Expulsion from the party was the most severe punishment because expelled party members were deprived of all the benefits of
party membership. Expulsion was reserved for obvious and severe
offenses. For example, when large amounts of an organization's
money were embezzled, the party member must be arrested and
prosecuted by the judicial system.[52] However, though expulsion
from the party must immediately follow a guilty verdict, this
seemingly simple rule was not universally applied. In some cases,
KPK, for their own reasons, did not turn cases over to the courts:
The chairman of the all-union trading agency, Torgsin, for example, was expelled from the party for self-provision and embezzlement, but the Bureau of KPK specifically noted that "it is not
expedient to pass this case to the court."[53]

An extreme case is presented by one Gassan-Ali-Omed, the
director of Brynzotrest cheese factory located in Moscow and subordinated to the Ministry of Food Industry, which was then
headed by Politburo member A. Mikoyan. Gassan-Ali-Omed
oversaw the production of low-quality production, sold at high
prices, while decreasing output. An audit revealed financial losses
and embezzlements of more than 3 million rubles. In addition,
several witnesses reported that Gassan refused to sign a contract
with the branch trade union; he blamed Soviet rule for creating

50. Ibid., ll. 88–115.
51. Ibid.
52. Ibid., d. 14, ll. 1–13; ibid., d. 15, ll. 88–115.
53. Ibid., d. 53, l. 69.

the poverty of the workers and thus excused thefts by workers.[54] This combination of crimes appeared to qualify Gassan-Ali-Omed for imprisonment. In September of 1934, the Bureau of KPK expelled Gassan-Ali-Omed from the party. One would presume that the career of Gassan was ruined forever, as would have happened to most party members with such a record. The records show that, surprisingly, this was not Gassan-Ali-Omed's first expulsion; he had already been expelled on April 1933 by his local party organization for a similar wrongdoing. Nevertheless just a few months later—September 1933—his party membership was restored, and the expulsion was changed to a stern reprimand by the minister Mikoyan, and he was warned that unless he changed his behavior he would be subject to further punishment. Upon his second expulsion by the Bureau of KPK in September of 1934, he submitted an appeal, and in November 1934, KPK again replaced expulsion by a stern reprimand, exactly as a year earlier.[55] The only plausible explanation for Gassan-Ali-Omed's success in reversing expulsions (and avoiding imprisonment) was that he was not a rank-and-file manager but enjoyed the support of powerful friends, who managed to bring him back to the party and let him keep his managerial position. Probably, they needed him as much as he needed them.

If the clique-based explanation of the punishment reversals implicit in the Gassan-Ali-Omed story is correct, then the all-powerful and supposedly independent KPK was not actually free in its decision making: Only those who were not valuable to the ruling clique or did not belong to it could become real subjects of discipline and law enforcement. Members of the elite, especially those with powerful protectors, received mild punishments.

The records of KPK provide two more apparent patterns for escaping punishment or having punishments reversed: first, creating a perception of no selfish motives in illegal actions was a good

54. Ibid., d. 36, ll. 146–52.
55. Ibid., d. 40, l. 151.

defensive strategy; second, it was advantageous to have a decent biographical record (for example, to come from a poor family, to serve in the Red Army, to be victimized in the past by the "enemy"—tsarist government, White Guards, or a former superior who was uncovered as a "counterrevolutionary"). Observed patterns of KPK punishment reversals imply not only the possibility of reprimand removal but also the restoration to party ranks after some period for virtually all expelled. The repeated catch phrases were "allow to reconsider the case in a year on a petition from the party cell," or "prohibit to occupy responsible positions for 2 (3) years," or "taking into account a considerable record of success in the economic front and the lack of selfish motives [and/ or sincere penitence] restore party membership."

CONCLUSIONS

In market economies, a "good" legal system spells out clearly what is legal and what is illegal and punishes lawbreakers in a systematic and predictable fashion, and all participants understand which crimes are more serious than others. The Soviet planned economy, although there were a constitution and criminal codes, worked under the assumption that the plan was the law. The managers of the economy's resources faced criminal charges if they failed to fulfill the plan. However, the plan-law was mutlidimensional and changed frequently. Even an honest manager could not hope to fulfill the plan without breaking rules. Falsification of capacity, charging prices in excess of official prices, declaring inputs defective, and especially unplanned product exchange were all standard managerial tools.

Managers were party members by and large, and only the party could discipline its own. The courts and militia could not be trusted to carry out the party's business; only the party itself. The party leadership relied on its party control commission, KPK, to dispense "justice."

This chapter demonstrates that the system's directors had to walk a fine line between leniency, which encouraged illegal behavior, and harsh punishments, which might impede the work of the production unit. If hard-line positions within KPK had been allowed to prevail, virtually all managers would have been dismissed, thrown out of the party, and jailed. The growing depreciation of reprimands, which were piling up in personnel records, shows the consequence of a punishment system in which virtually all participants are "guilty" in one way or another. If the pragmatists within KPK had prevailed, virtually all offenders would have gone unpunished because their intentions were "good" or their failure was the fault of others. It is therefore no wonder that KPK justice was dispensed unevenly, subjectively, and arbitrarily.

The Soviet justice system was supposedly based on the precedent principle.[56] Exemplary cases were published in the Soviet press to serve as instructions to others. However, these exemplary cases did not set precedents. They were dictated by the government and party rather than by rulings of an independent court. Precedents were short-lived, since they were frequently overridden by subsequent decrees. It was hard for both controllers and managers to learn rules of behavior from them. This chapter does, however, reveal certain patterns. One is the great willingness of KPK officials to look the other way in the case of managers who fulfilled the production plan, even production plans reduced by falsifications of enterprise capacity. A second feature is the importance of high-level protection, which seemed to overwhelm the purported independence of KPK. A third feature is the surprising willingness to pardon offenders, even in the case of serious crimes.

The Soviet economic system of the 1930s, much like its contemporary successor in modern-day Russia, lacked a conventional "rule of law." The fact that it survived and functioned for sixty years suggests that it had informal rules and practices that were sufficiently well understood by the participants. No matter how

56. The Criminal Code. Moscow, 1938, p. 174.

well entrenched these informal practices were, the lives of managers must have been subject to enormous uncertainty and arbitrariness and their documented reactions (forming protective networks, striving for economic autonomy, seeking stability outside the formal system) were the consequence.

8 STALIN'S LAST PLAN

Aleksei Tikhonov and
Paul R. Gregory

The Soviet Union entered the postwar period as a major contributor to the Allied victory over Hitler's Germany. The presence of Soviet troops was used to create a new Soviet empire, covering most of Central and Southeastern Europe. The communist party was victorious in China. The Soviet economic system had survived the crises of the 1930s and had provided most of the resources to defeat the Nazi war machine. World War II spelled the end of colonial empires, leaving poor countries in Asia and Africa free to choose between democratic capitalism and Soviet socialism. The Soviets' promise of rapid economic growth held considerable appeal for such poor countries. The Stalinist system was put in place in the early 1930s amid confusion, experimentation, and a conviction that industrialization must take place quickly. This hastily conceived economic system (described in earlier chapters) had demanded much of the population in terms of sacrifice, hunger, and political terror.

Since its inception, Soviet leaders had not had a period of normalcy in which to consider how the system should work under "normal" conditions. As the Soviet Union entered the postwar era, at long last it had an opportunity to reevaluate its priorities and to make changes in the economic and political system it had

The authors are grateful to the Hoover Institution for its support of this project.

cobbled together in the 1930s. The immediate postwar period, 1945–1950, was not a time for such reflection. Planning priorities were simple— recovery from wartime destruction. The first postwar plan, the Fourth Five-Year Plan (1945–1950), restored most branches to their prewar levels, with most resources going to those with the most war damage.

RETHINKING THE SYSTEM AFTER THE WAR?

Stalin and the Communist Party had used party congresses to address weighty issues. The prewar history of the Soviet Communist Party shows that party congresses were convened only after internal power struggles had been resolved. For example, the XVI Party Congress of 1930 was delayed until Stalin's conclusive victory over his remaining potent rivals within the Politburo (Bukharin and Rykov). This congress stilled opposition to the Stalin leadership and embarked on a course of temporary partial liberalization.[1] The convening of the first postwar party congress would therefore signal that the internal power struggle concerning Stalin's eventual successor had been resolved (Stalin died in March of 1953) and that the party leadership was ready to take on major issues. The convening of the XIX Party Congress in 1952, thirteen years after the XVIII Congress in 1939, indicated a new political equilibrium and the party's readiness to address issues of postwar economic and political strategy.

The published official record of the XIX Party Congress is relatively uninformative.[2] We are fortunate, however, to have the secret file of all documents relating to the XIX Congress, preserved in a special fond, which includes the very first discussions

---

1. For an account of this period, see O. V. Khlevnyuk, *Politburo: Mekhanizm politicheskoi vlasti v 1930-e gody* (Moscow: Rosspen, 1996).

2. *Direktivy XIX Sezda partii po piatomu piatiletnemu planu razvitiia SSSR na 1951–1955 gody* (Moscow: Gosudarstvennoe izdatelstvo politicheskoi literatury, 1952); *Ob itogakh vypolneniia piatovogo piatiletnego plana razvitiia SSSR i soiuznykh respublik na 1951–1955 gody* (Moscow: Gosudarstvennoe izdatelstvo politicheskoi literatury, 1956).

of convening the congress, all preparatory documents, drafts of speeches and reports, as well as the plans and reports drawn up by planning agencies for use in the congress. These documents were circulated to a limited group of the highest state and party officials; most were addressed directly to Stalin, who at that time was chairman of the Council of Ministers (the head of government) and General Secretary of the Communist Party. This chapter is largely based on the XIX Party Congress file located in the archives of the Hoover Institution.[3] This fond contains all materials associated with the preparation and execution of the XIX Party Congress, including the preparatory documents for the Fifth Five-Year Plan, which constituted its most important agenda item. The XIX Party Congress fond permits us to look behind the scenes of the Party Congress. We pay special attention to the reasons for the lengthy delay in convening the congress and to the preparation of the Fifth Five-Year Plan, which constituted the first real opportunity to reexamine economic priorities for the postwar era.

The Five-Year Delay

The Hoover archives reveal the little-known intent of the Politburo to call the XIX Party Congress at the beginning of 1947, assigning A. Zhdanov the major organizational role. At this time, Zhdanov was second only to Stalin in the party, heading its secretariat. This Politburo assignment clearly established Zhdanov as Stalin's intended successor. On January 7, 1947, the Politburo approved a decision to call a plenum of the Central Committee on February 21, which included as a main agenda item the convocation of the XIX Party Congress and assigned Zhdanov responsi-

3. XIX Congress file (RTsHINDI, fond 592, 113 files) is a collection of documents very different in origin, all documents that had any connection to or made any reference to the XIX Party Congress. This collection came to the Hoover Institution archives as a part of a joint Hoover-Rosarchiv project and is located in films 2.2590–2.2602.

bility for the agenda.[4] The XIX Party Congress was eventually convened five years later under the direction of G. Malenkov, Zhdanov's rival. Why the five-year delay?

The January 1947 Central Committee plenum was only the second meeting of the Central Committee since 1941. Following the January 1947 plenum, there was a seven-month break, until August 15, when a short meeting took place to approve the Politburo decision to call the XIX Congress. Official descriptions of this meeting describe primarily discussions of agricultural issues with no mention of the convocation of the XIX Party Congress, which was (again following the Politburo's directive) to be the main item on the Plenum's agenda.[5] The official records, therefore, conceal the fact that the calling of the XIX Party Congress was discussed in 1947, but Zhdanov's personal collection of materials does indeed contain his speech at the 1947 plenum, in which he proposed a new party program and a new party statute as the main items of the XIX Party Congress agenda. He scheduled the congress to take place at the end of 1947 or at least in 1948.[6] The XIX Party Congress archives then fall silent without a single mention of the XIX Congress until December 1951, when the Politburo again set the date for the Congress for October of 1952.[7]

The delay in calling the party congress, although ignored in official accounts, caused apprehension among party members, as reflected in a note from a party member: "I request that you give an answer as to why a congress has not been called for so long. There are harmful rumors, such as this is Stalin's last congress . . . that he is aging."[8] Although there is no official explanation for the five-year delay in calling the congress, the answer lies in the fact that party congresses cannot be called in the midst of internal

4. Hoover film 2.2590 (592-1-1)
5. See Khrushchev's detailed description in N.S. Khrushchev, *Vospominania: Vremya. Liudi. Vlast'* (Moskovskie Novosti, 1999), p. 12–13.
6. Zhdanov's Personal Fond, 77-3-173.
7. Film 2.2590 (592-1-1), Protocol N 84, December 7, 1951, Meeting.
8. Film 2.2592(592-1-27), Letters to XIX CPSU Congress.

dissension within the Politburo. The power struggle that delayed the XIX Party Congress was the intense battle over Stalin's successor.

The Succession Struggle

Stalin, owing to declining health and perhaps declining interest, was no longer in active control of the economy and of his subordinates at the turn of the decade of the 1950s. He spent less time in Moscow and more time in the south, receiving fewer and fewer visitors. "As is shown by Stalin's appointments journal for meetings in his Kremlin office, the circle of his appointments diminished. If he met with 2,000 visitors in 1940, then in 1950 the number diminished to around 700, and in 1951 and 1952, less than 500 per year. He did not appear for months in his Kremlin office. In 1950 he did not receive visitors for almost five months."[9] Stalin himself mentioned the succession issue, at least in principle. One of the few surviving senior party leaders from the purges of the 1930s, L. Kaganovich, stated: "Stalin generally considered that comrades should drop the task of direct rule after reaching the age of seventy. They can be advisers but not rulers."[10]

Stalin's successor was not to be drawn from the old political elite that survived the Great Purges. By the end of the war, the old political elite had shrunk to four: V. Molotov, K. Voroshilov, A. Mikoyan, and L. Kaganovich. This group appeared to be more interested in its physical survival than in power and did not appear to represent a cohesive political force. It had been generally regarded that Molotov, on account of his earlier experience as prime minister and foreign minister (somehow Stalin thought that the prime minister had to be Russian in origin), would be Stalin's successor, but Stalin effectively removed Molotov (along with Mi-

---

9. R. Pikhoia, "Sotsialno-politicheskoe razvitie i bor'ba za vlast' v poslevoennom Sovetskom Soiuze (1945–1953)," MIZh, no. 6 (1999); http://www.machaon. ru/.

10. Ibid., p. 498.

koyan) from contention.[11] Khrushchev wrote in his memoirs: "Whereas earlier we, people of the prewar times, had regarded Molotov as the future leader of the country after Stalin's death, we now understood that that would not be the case. At every regular meeting, Stalin attacked Molotov, attacked Mikoyan, devouring them. These two were in disgrace; their very lives were in danger."[12]

To replace the ranks of the old leaders depleted by the Great Terror, Stalin brought in new faces to the Politburo. Although Stalin had earlier refrained from consolidating party and state power, he himself assumed the chairmanship of the Council of Ministers in 1940 in addition to his position as General Secretary of the Communist Party. He added five younger party leaders: Beria, Voznesensky, Zhdanov, Kosygin, and Khrushchev; they would vie to become Stalin's successor after the war. These new leaders were assigned different responsibilities: Zhdanov, Voznesensky, and Kosygin were assigned party, ideology, and planning; Beria and Malenkov, who served together on the State Committee for Defense (GKO) during the war, were responsible for the military and security. Zhdanov served as the head of the party apparatus. Malenkov became Stalin's deputy and eventually deputy prime minister. Voznesensky also served as deputy prime minister, carrying out the lion's share of work in the state apparatus, including the chairmanship of the State Planning Commission (Gosplan). According to a Politburo decree of March 29, 1948, Vozensensky and Malenkov alternatively chaired meetings of the Council of Ministers. They formed two competing groups—Zhdanov-Voznesensky (also known as the Leningrad group) and Malenkov-Beria—that engaged in the war of succession.

Zhdanov, the former first secretary of Leningrad and member of Politburo since 1939, served as secretary of the Party's Central Committee and was clearly second only to Stalin in the party or-

11. Khrushchev, *Vospominania*, p. 96.
12. Ibid.

ganization in the late 1940s. It was in this capacity that the Politburo assigned him in February 1947 to make preparations for the
XIX Party Congress. Apparently, the counterweight of his rivals
Malenkov and Beria stalemated the first call for a party congress.
Eighteen months later, before any congress had been convened,
Zhdanov died (August 31, 1948), from an apparent heart attack,
although foul play cannot be ruled out. Zhdanov's death dis-
rupted the fragile political equilibrium and initiated a series of
political events that led to the defeat of surviving members of his
Leningrad group, of which Voznesensky remained the most influential. First, three prominent Leningrad party officials were accused of anti-party activities. In February 1949, Malenkov, the
main rival of the Leningrad group, was sent to Leningrad to investigate, where he ordered arrests. Voznesensky, though not directly
implicated, was faulted for lack of vigilance and in September
1949 was fired as head of Gosplan after a series of setbacks engineered by his opponents, starting with an accusation of having
deliberately disobeyed an order of Stalin.[13] Voznesensky's fate

13. Oleg Khlevnyuk, "Sovetskaia ekonomicheskaia politika na rubezhe 40–50
godov i delo gosplana," Working Paper, Florence, Italy, March 2000, describes the
power struggle as follows: In November of 1948, Stalin proposed that Voznesensky
work out a plan to eliminate the usual seasonality of the first quarter. According to
Mikoyan, Voznesensky agreed, even though he knew this was an impossible task.
Voznesensky agreed to the necessary increases in the first-quarter production plan,
but the plan change was never made. Pomaznev (the head of Gossnab) informed
Stalin in February as part of the attack on Voznesensky. Stalin gave an order to the
Council of Ministers to investigate, and it sided with Pomaznev. Beria, through his
agent in Gosplan, found a memo of Voznesensky stating that it was unrealistic to
eliminate seasonality of the first quarter—and wrote on it "v delo" (in processing),
which effectively stopped the order. Beria placed this memo on Stalin's desk on
March 5, 1949. A 1949 decree "About Gosplan," which bears marks of Stalin's
participation, states: "The government of the USSR not once declared that the most
important task of Gosplan is the assurance in state plans of the growth and development of the economy, as indicated by existing reserves of productive capacity and
battling against any kind of agency tendency toward lowering of plans. As the general state organ for planing the national economy, Gosplan must be an absolutely
objective and one hundred percent honest organ. In its work, there should be no
kind of influence or manipulation of figures. On the basis of an investigation of the
Bureau of the Council of Ministers, it was established that Gosplan allows nonobjec-
tive and dishonest approaches to the questions of planning and evaluation of plan

was sealed when his opponents fabricated a case showing that Gosplan had mishandled secret documents. He was arrested along with a number of his relatives and was executed on October 1, 1950, on the basis of the directive "On responsibility for distribution of government secrets and loss of documents containing government secrets." The ensuing 1949 purge of Gosplan was narrow, showing that Voznesensky, not Gosplan, was the real target. There was no general accusation of counterrevolutionary groups within Gosplan; of Gosplan's 1,400 employees, 130 were fired and more than forty of those were transferred to other work; of twelve deputies of Voznesensky, only one was imprisoned.

The Soviet leadership thus entered the 1950s with the Malenkov-Beria group victorious as a consequence of the physical elimination of Zhdanov and Voznesensky and with an ailing Stalin. The Politburo announced the convening of the long-awaited XIX Party Congress in December 1951 and named Malenkov to deliver the keynote address.

THE XIX PARTY CONGRESS

The "new call" for the XIX Party Congress reflected the outcome of the succession struggle between the Malenkov-Beria faction and the defeated Leningrad faction. Whereas Zhdanov had announced the agenda of the XIX Party Congress in 1947, the 1952 agenda gave Malenkov the highly visible role of delivering the keynote address, while Stalin limited himself to a short appearance. The Hoover fond contains copies of the various draft versions of Malenkov's speech along with the version that was actually delivered, and various commentaries on Malenkov's draft speech, especially those by Stalin, permit us to determine the degree of consensus and particularly Stalin's own stance. We

---

fulfillment, which expresses itself in the manipulation of figures with the goal of obscuring the real state of affairs. It was also discovered that Gosplan has joined ranks with separate ministries and agencies to lower productive capacities and economic plans of ministries."

know from Khrushchev how carefully Stalin prepared his papers and speeches. [14] It was therefore to be expected that Stalin would review the important Malenkov address with great care.

In his memoirs, Kaganovich confirmed that there was widespread discussion of the Malenkov report: "The draft version of Malenkov's speech was discussed under the direction of Stalin on the presidium and several times corrections were made."[15] The XIX Congress file contains the version of Malenkov's report on which Stalin's corrections and handwritten comments were made.[16] It is noteworthy that these comments were largely editorial in nature, although some of them obviously reveal differences in Stalin's and Malenkov's views. First, Stalin edited to "soften" Malenkov's critical tone concerning the failures of the economy. He deleted adjectives like "frequent" or "numerous" as applied to errors and mistakes in the economy; "numerous" cases of bad-quality production became "cases of bad-quality production."[17] Second, Stalin showed his flair for colorful terminology: Malenkov's "evil persons who want to overthrow the regime" became Stalin's "those who want to stab us in the back."[18] Third, Stalin deleted some references to "Stalin-hero," but he left many such references untouched; he cut two pages glorifying Stalin at the end of the report and put the word "Party" in place of "Stalin." Fourth, Stalin made a number of modest corrections to Malenkov's suggested control figures for the fifth five-year plan (as reported in the chapter by Gregory). Stalin's relatively modest corrections can be interpreted as putting more "social optimism" into Malenkov's speech and as confirming that everything was under control. The best example of the latter is Stalin's editing

14. N. Khrushchev, *Vospominania*, p. 109.

15. L. Kaganovich, *Pamyatnie zapiski* (Moscow:Vagrius, 1996), p. 492.

16. Hoover 2.2590 (592-1-4, 5, 6, 7, 8, 9). All these files contain different versions of Malenkov's report, officially called Otchetniy Doklad TsK. File 7 contains Stalin's corrections, dated July 17, 1952.

17. 2.2590 (592-1-6). Subsequent citations give only the pages of the report (following the archival pagination).

18. 2.2590 (592-1-6).

of Malenkov's "After the war the inflow of new party members slowed" to Stalin's "The Party decided to slow down the recruitment of new party members." The only case in which Malenkov did not accept Stalin's correction, with respect to the "social optimism" issue, was the passage on the role of satire in Soviet literature where Malenkov insisted that Soviet artists must "with the fire of satire burn out of Soviet life everything that is negative, rotten, dead." Stalin probably thought it was too harsh a method to be used in optimistic Soviet literature.[19]

Malenkov's report to the XIX Party Congress covered foreign policy, internal policy, and party issues. The speech failed to break new ground, but it did raise the notion of peaceful coexistence; among the traditional invectives against the "American imperialism," Malenkov said: "We are confident that, in peaceful competition with capitalism, the socialist system will prove its superiority more strikingly with each passing year. But we have no intention whatever of forcing our ideology or our economic system on anybody. The export of revolution is nonsense, says Comrade Stalin. Each country will make its own revolution if it wants to do so, and if it does not want to do so there will be no revolution."[20] Malenkov was also critical of economic performance, stating, for example, that as a consequence of "unsatisfactory utilization of production capacity and extensive waste due to mismanagement, many industrial enterprises fail to fulfill their assignments in lowering unit cost of output and greatly exceed their quotas of expenditure."[21] In his discussion of the party, Malenkov focused on the need for more inner-party democracy and self-criticism: "The Central Committee has focused the attention

19. In 1955, Khrushchev used this episode in his latter power struggle against Malenkov, causing additional documents on this issue to be placed in the XIX Congress file.

20. English translation here is taken from *Current Soviet Policies: The Documentary Record of the Nineteenth Communist Party Congress and the Reorganization After Stalin's Death* (New York: Praeger, 1953), p. 102.

21. Ibid., p. 113.

of Party organizations on the task of consistently practicing inner Party democracy and developing criticism and self-criticism."[22]

The Fifth Five-Year Plan: The Main Agenda Item

Party congresses require a major theme. If the XIX Party Congress had taken place as originally scheduled in 1947 under Zhdanov, its theme would have been the new party program. Under Malenkov-Beria, the major theme became the ratification of the second postwar five-year plan—the fifth five-year plan—for the period 1951–1955. It is for this reason that the XIX Party Congress fond contains extremely rich materials on the origins and preparation of the fifth five-year plan.

The USSR learned that it was living in the fifth five-year plan when *Pravda* published the agenda of the XIX Congress on August 20, 1952. The state's official economic publication—*Planned Economy*—had not included a single reference to a new five-year plan during the period 1949–1952, and the announcement of the existence of the fifth five-year plan in the fourth number of this journal in 1952 was entirely unexpected. Western experts long speculated on the causes of these delays. Naum Jasny suggested that as late as 1951 there was no five-year plan at all, probably because of the Korean War and Stalin's lack of interest. [23] Eugène Zaleski speculated that Gosplan had proposed drafting a long-term plan in the summer of 1947 but that project was abandoned because of the firing of Voznesensky as head of Gosplan, Stalin's own ambitious plans for building communism through large construction projects, and the Korean War.[24]

PREPARATION OF THE FIFTH FIVE-YEAR PLAN

The Hoover archives allow us to trace the chronology of the Fifth Five-Year Plan. Its first draft was prepared already at the end of

22. Ibid., p. 117.
23. Naum Jasny, *Soviet Industrialization, 1928–1952* (Chicago: University of Chicago Press, 1961), p. 250.
24. Eugène Zaleski, *Stalinist Planning for Economic Growth, 1933–1952* (Chapel Hill: University of North Carolina Press, 1980), pp. 395–96.

May/beginning of June of 1950—half a year before the formal end of the preceding Fourth Five-Year Plan and almost two years before the calling of the XIX Party Congress. At this time, M. Saburov, the chairman of Gosplan and successor to the executed Voznesensky, submitted three plan documents addressed to Stalin: Report of Gosplan (M. Z. Saburov) "On the draft directives for preparing the plan of the economy for 1951–1955 prepared by order of the Council of Ministers of the USSR," Draft Decree of the Council of Ministers "On directives for the preparation of the five-year plan for the development of the economy for 1951–1955," and statistical appendixes including the basic indicators for industry.[25]

The June 1950 draft was prepared by Gosplan for ratification by the Council of Ministers; since, as of June 1950, there was no intent to call a new party congress, Gosplan assumed that Council of Ministers (and of course Politburo) ratification would be all that was necessary. The June 1950 Gosplan plan focused on the problems of plan fulfillment from 1946 to 1950: the electricity deficit and its resolution, the need to develop machinery, the oil deficit, the types of machinery to be developed, and rail construction. The 1950 Gosplan report also focused on problems of incomplete capital construction and the failure to reduce construction costs, resulting in incomplete construction. In general, one can say that the 1950 Gosplan draft was a typical five-year plan document that differed little in form and content from earlier five-year plans; in fact, its format perfectly mirrored that of the Fourth Five-Year Plan.[26]

The XIX Party Congress fond contains all subsequent five-year plan drafts arranged chronologically, allowing us to trace the manner in which long-term Soviet plans were formulated and

25. File 16 (2.2591) (592-1-16) contains the original draft of the plan dated June 3, 1950.

26. "Zakon o pyateletnem plane vosstanovlenia i razvitiia narodnogo khoziaistva SSSR na 1946–1950" in *Bor'ba KPSS za vosstanovlenie i razvitie narodnogo khoziaistva v poslevoennom periode (1945–1953)* (Moscow: Gospolitizdat, 1961), pp. 47–119.

passed through various state organizations prior to their approval by political authorities. This process allows us to understand the various interest groups at play during the planning process, how they affected the process, and with what success.

The Process

The first draft of the fifth five-year plan was completed on or around the end of May 1950 (see chronology in Table 1). It was finally approved by the Politburo on June 23, 1952, and by the XIX Party Congress on October 14, 1952. In other words, the process of preparation and approval of the fifth five-year plan took more than two years. What happened in this interval? What was the internal process?

We begin by noting two regularities: first, at least at the formal level, all discussions were based on Gosplan drafts, which served as the starting point for all deliberations; second, there appeared to be no direct channel of communication between the main planners. All communications were directed to Stalin, and the various planning bodies would then react to the others' positions directly to Stalin. The Gosplan drafts served as the basis for the discussion of the five-year plan drafts by the two most important alternate planning agencies—the State Supply Agency, Gossnab, headed by one of Stalin's oldest associates, Kaganovich, and the Ministry of Finance, headed by longtime minister Zverev.

A number of conclusions can be drawn based on the chronology of draft plans shown in Table 1. First, the five-year planning process required a great deal of time. The initial Gosplan draft was completed in early summer of 1950 and the final approval at the XIX Party Congress was on October 14, 1952—a time span of more than two years. The chronology shows the vast number of steps in the process, with Gosplan alone submitting eighteen separate documents (plans), Gossnab eight plans, and the Ministry of Finance two commentaries. Second, the chronology shows three major rounds of discussion: May–June 1950, January 1951,

TABLE 1

CHRONOLOGY OF THE FIFTH FIVE-YEAR PLAN

Date	Agency	Document	Title
1950			
May 31	Gossnab	Reference material	Tables of the volume of industrial production
May 31	Gossnab	Note	Note of the Chairman of Gossnab
June 3	Gosplan	Report	Report of Gosplan about draft directives
June 3	Gosplan	Draft	Decree of Council of Ministers "About the directives for preparing a plan for the national economy for 1951–55"
June 3	Gosplan	Supplements	Basic indicators of the development of the national economy for 1951–1955
June 8	Gosplan	Notes	Notes of the chairman of Gosplan about the conclusions of Gossnab, Ministry of Finance, and others
June 9	State Labor Committee	Notes	Commentaries of State Labor Committee
June 23	Ministry of Finance	Notes	Commentaries of Ministry of Finance
1951			
Jan. 23	Gosplan	Draft	Decree of Central Committee "About the directives for preparing the 5th five-year plan"
Jan. 23	Gosplan	Report	"About the directives for preparing the 5th five-year plan for 1951–55"
Jan. 23	Gosplan	Notes	Military and special branches of industry
Feb. 2	Gossnab	Draft	Draft decree of the Council of Ministers about the economizing of lead in the national economy (with Stalin's comments)
Feb. 2	Gossnab	Notes	About the draft of Gosplan "About the directives for preparing the 5th five-year plan of the national economy"
Mar. 2	Gossnab	Notes	Note of Kaganovich about the volume of accumulation and state reserves
June 7	Gosplan	Informational material	Basic indicators of the national economy
June 7	Gosplan	Report	About the draft of directives for creating the 5th five-year plan of development 1951–55

Date	Institution	Type	Description
June 7	**Gosplan**	Appendix	Basic developments of indicators to the draft for preparing the directives for preparing the plan
June 7	**Gosplan**	Informational material	Basic indicators of development of the national economy according to economic regions
June 7	**Gosplan**	Informational material	Basic indicators for the development of the most important electrical systems
June 7	**Gosplan**	Supplement	Basic corrections to the draft directives for preparing the 5th five-year plan presented to the Council of Ministers in January 1951
June 7	Gosplan	Notes	Notes of Saburov concerning the military and special branches of the economy
June 7	Gosplan	Informational materials	Basic indicators of the 5th five-year plan of the development of the national economy
June 7	Gosplan	Draft	Decree of the Central Committee "About the directives for preparing the 5th five-year plan"
July 17	**Gossnab**	Notes	About the draft directives for preparing the 5th five-year plan
July 17	**Gossnab**	Informational materials	Preliminary balances
July 17	Gossnab	Informational materials	Tables of resources and requirements
July 27	**Ministry of Finance**	Notes	Commentary of Ministry of Finance
Aug. 16	Gosplan	Notes	On the draft decree of the Council of Ministers and the Central Committee "Directives . . ."
Aug. 16	**Gosplan**	Draft	Decree of the Council of Ministers and the Central Committee "Directives to the preparation of the 5th five-year plan"
1952 June 23	Politburo	Decision	To prepare "Directives for preparing the 5th five-year plan"
Aug. 15	**Central Committee**	Decision	Decision of Plenum of Central Committee to approve the draft "Directives"
Aug. 20	Central Committee	Draft	Publication of directives in *Pravda*
Oct. 14	Party Congress	**Directives**	Directives of the XIX Party Congress for the 5th five-year plan for the development of the USSR for 1951–55

NOTE: Gossnab apparently used different dating procedures for its files. The Gossnab commentaries refer to the Gosplan drafts dated later than the Gossnab commentaries.

173

and June 1951. There is no evidence of discussion of the fourth project of August 1951, which appeared in the official Politburo–Council of Ministers document but was not approved. The final "Directives" approved by the XIX Party Congress in October 1952 was basically the same document as proposed one year earlier.

Third, the various planning agencies responded quickly to the other draft plans. The long intervals of inactivity appear to be explained by the delays of political authorities in pushing the process along. These delays cannot be attributed to the need to wait for the convening of the XIX Party Congress, because initially it was expected that this plan would be ratified by the Council of Ministers–Politburo without any benediction by a party congress. Actual approval of the Fifth Five-Year Plan occurred with the decision of the central committee to approve the plan on August 15, 1952, almost two months before the formal approval by the XIX Party Congress.

Stalin's Minor Role

Archival materials relating to the 1930s show Stalin's intense involvement in five-year planning; Stalin was still actively involved in planning as late as the 1949 annual plan (see the chapter by Gregory). We can get some sense of Stalin's involvement in the Fifth Five-Year Plan from his written comments and his other communications relating to this five-year plan. All the draft plans and agency discussions are addressed directly to Stalin; the number of copies was limited and all are marked "completely secret," with the detailed defense budget marked "especially secret." In the Hoover files, although some documents are accompanied by notes that indicate corrections made by Stalin himself, usually in the form of markings and handwritten comments, few of the documents contain any sign of Stalin's own corrections; there are only underline marks indicating that the text had been read. Stalin's few remarks reveal his preferences. In a rare example of personal intervention, Stalin marked clearly his preference for military over consumer production, when he demanded an increase in aluminum production for aviation and a decrease in "civilian output."[27] In another isolated comment, Stalin asked about the possibility of decreasing coal imports. Few though they are, these remarks reinforce the standard image of a dictator concerned with the creation of a heavy industry base, self-sufficient from capitalist economies.

Our conclusion is that we do not see the same type of intense involvement by Stalin in the Fifth Five-Year Plan as in the five-year plans of the 1930s. A number of explanations can be offered, ranging from Stalin's growing interest in long-term technological plans, his realization that five-year plans really did not matter, or the simple fact that Stalin was ill and old and not up to the time-consuming job of reviewing all these statistical calculations.

The Battle among Agencies

In the prewar period, no single organization handled supply. Supply contracts were formulated in general terms by Gosplan and the contracts themselves were handled by producer supply organizations or specialized supply organizations. The most important change in the management of the economy was the formation of the State Committee for Material and Equipment Supply (Gossnab) on December 15, 1947.[28] Gossnab was set up to organize the distribution of materials among major wholesale users, such as ministries and territorial organizations. To add

27. Memo of Kaganovich to Stalin ("Ob ekonomii svintsa"), 592-1-19.

28. Kaganovich wrote (*Pamyatuie zapiski*, p. 494) about the founding of Gossnab: "In the end of 1947, Stalin proposed to the Politburo to split Gosplan into two different agencies—Gosnab and Gossnab. Gossnab was to be the independent distributor of all state resources. As justification, Stalin pointed out the growing complexity of the economy. The director of Gossnab was supposed to be one of the deputy chairmen of the Council of Ministers and a member of Politburo. The administrative core of the new agency was mostly transferred from former functional supply agencies—Glavneftsbyt, Glavmetallsbyt, Glavuglesbyt, Glavlessbyt, and Glavkhimsbyt."

weight to Gossnab, one of Stalin's most experienced aides, L. Kaganovich, was named the first director of Gossnab. Gossnab's most important task was to battle the ministries' struggle for excess materials by working out "scientific" norms of materials usage. Beginning in 1948, Gossnab proposed 1800 norms for industry; by 1950, it was using 6000 norms.[29]

Gossnab was thus added to Gosplan and to the Ministry of Finance as the third organization responsible for planning. Importantly, the five-year planning process did not provide a formal venue for the industrial ministries to react to the proposals of Gosplan, as they most obviously did in the case of annual plans. In the five-year planning process only designated state committees were allowed to present their commentaries on Gosplan's drafts.[30] The agency commentaries were signed by the heads of the three agencies, Saburov (Gosplan), Kaganovich (Gossnab), and Zverev (Ministry of Finance), but some specialized reports were signed by department heads. All documents were addressed directly to Stalin; therefore, there was no formal channel from one agency to another (although informal channels may have existed).

Gosplan

Table 2 shows five drafts of the Fifth Five-Year Plan. The core of Gosplan's five-year plan drafts were the physical targets for 127 products (1955 end targets with 1950 figures given for reference). These products included coal, steel, number of automobiles, locomotives, tons of grain and milk products, and so on. Gosplan also provided aggregate figures for national income, gross industrial production (broken down into sectors A and B), gross agricultural production, and the cumulated total of capital

29. E. Lokshinam, "Normirovanie raskhoda syriia i materialov v proizvodstve," *Planovoe khoziaistvo*, no. 6, 1950.

30. Other state committees were also permitted a say, such as the Central Statistical Administration, the State Technology Committee, the State Construction Committee, and the Central Committee of Trade Unions.

Table 2
Physical Targets of the Drafts of the Fifth Five-Year Plan
(June 1950; January, June, and August 1951)

Nomenclature	Measure	GP (6/50)	GS (6/50)	MF (6/50)	GP (1/51)	GS (1/51)	GP (6/51)	MF (6/51)	GP 8/51	Final-1952 (Congress)	Results GKS-1957
Pig iron	Mln.tons	31	36.5		33	36	36		33.3	33.88	33.3
Steel	Mln.tons	41.5	47		42.7	47.4	46.1		43.2	44.29	45.3
Rolled steel	Mln.tons	31.5	36		32.5		35.2		33	34.04	35.3
Small-section steel	Mln.tons		2.4			2.3	2.3		2.2	2.29	
Plate steel	Mln.tons		3.8			3.9	3.9		3.6	3.79	
Wire rod	Mln.tons		2.3			1.8	1.8		1.75		
Carbon steel, sheet	Mln.tons		1.4								
Carbon steel, sort	Mln.tons		2.7								
Alloyed sort	Mln.tons		1.75								
Structural steel	Mln.tons		0.135						0.06	0.07	
Calibrated steel	Mln.tons		0.85								
Reinforcing iron	Mln.tons		0.7								
Broad-brimmed girders	Mln.tons		0.4								
Low-alloyed rolled steel	Mln.tons		0.3								
High-carbon wire	Mln.tons		0.08								
Steel pipes	Mln.tons	4	4.3		3.65				3.5		
Steel pipes, casing	Mln.tons	0.726	611								
Steel pipes, drilling	Mln.tons	0.171	147								
Steel pipes, pump-compressors	Mln.tons	0.226	215								
Steel pipes, oil pipelines	Mln.tons	0.144	380								
Steel pipes, cracking	Th.tons	43	43								
Steel pipes, rolled	Mln.tons		0.6								
Steel pipes, seamless rolled	Mln.tons		0.26								
Steel pipes, ball-bearing	Mln.tons		0.15								
Coke	Mln.tons	46	51		48.2	51			47		43.6
Coke-metallurgy	Mln.tons		45								

TABLE 2 (continued)

Nomenclature	Measure	GP (6/50)	GS (6/50)	MF (6/50)	GP (1/51)	GS (1/51)	GP (6/51)	MF (6/51)	GP 8/51	Final-1952 (Congress)	Results GKS-1957
Iron ore	Mln.tons	65.8			74.1		80		75		71.9
Aluminium	Mln.tons	0.4	0.5		0.5	0.57	0.5		0.5	406.25	
Copper	Mln.tons	0.49	0.6						0.44		
Refined copper	Mln.tons	0.4	0.545		0.46	0.62	0.46		0.44	2,387.43	
Lead	Mln.tons	0.325	0.325		0.325		0.325		0.275	278.09	
Zink	Mln.tons	0.4	0.4		0.4				0.35		
Magnesium	Th.tons	18							18		
Tin	Th.tons	20	20		17		17		15	12.05	
Nickel	Th.tons	39	69		59	70			60	59.23	
Tungsten	Th.tons		15				18		16		
Molybdenum	Th.tons		5.7			8.9	11		9		
Cobalt	Th.tons		1.1			1.15	1.2		1.2		
Stibium	Th.tons		4.3								
Stibium-electrolyte	Th.tons		3.2								
Electric power	Bln.kWh	167	170		169	175	175		166.5	163.77	170.2
Hydroelectric power	Bln.kWh	32	35				32				23.2
Electric power—Ural	Bln.kWh		31.5				27.4				
Electric power—Kemerovo	Bln.kWh		7								
Electric power—Central region	Bln.kWh		31				26.5				
Electric power—South	Bln.kWh		23.4				24.2				
Electric power—Uzbek.	Bln.kWh		3.36								
Coal	Mln.tons	378	400		384	410	384		370	372.61	391.3
Coal-coke	Mln.tons		92						82	77.36	
Peat	Mln.tons	47	47		46				44	44.70	50.8
Petroleum	Mln.tons	60	60		60		60		60	70.25	70.8
Gas	Bln.cbm	13.552	10.7		10.7						10.356
Metal cutting machines	Th.pieces	90	90		90		80		72		117.1
Metal cutting machines—large, heavy, and single-design types	Th.pieces	3.9	4.3		4	4.344	4.3		4.3	3.99	3.54

Item	Unit							
Instruments	Mln.rub	2,850				3,500	4,108.70	
Vacuum instruments	Mln.pieces					100		
Metallurgical equipment	Th.tons	200	220.5	200	232	225	210.23	172.1
Steam and gas turbines	Mln.qW	6.84	6.84	6.2	6.235	5.9	5,428.00	4.069
Hydraulic turbines	Mln.qW	1.93	1.6	2.77	2.699	2.58	2,454.15	1.4919
Boilers	Th.sqm	1,000		962	992	900	964.29	
Boilers—high capacity	Th.sqm	315	315					
Steam turbine generators	Mln.qW	3.2	5	3.35	3.5	3.2		3.113
Hydraulic turbine generators	Mln.qW	1.8				2.8		1.4127
Power transformers	Mln.kW	20	20	25	28	26		
Electric motors (AC)	Mln.kW	11.5			27	11		
Electric motors (less than 100 w.)	Mln.pieces		1.75					
Electric motors (more than 100 w.)	Th.pieces	23	30	23		315		12.5
Cable	Th.tons	350		310	329	400	436.36	445.3
Motor vehicles	Th.pieces	700	700	450		400		329
Trucks	Th.pieces	555	555	362				
Trucks with gas generators	Th.pieces		120					
Trucks with gas balons	Th.pieces		60					
Dump trucks	Th.pieces		132					
Diesel trucks (7–10 tons)	Th.pieces		16					
Diesel trucks (10–12 tons)	Th.pieces		4.2					
Tractors	Th.pieces	190	190	129	163.5	225	135.23	163.4
Tractors (15 hp)	Th.pieces	396.76				277		321.8
Tractors—gas generators	Th.pieces	28	28					
Agricultural machines	Mln.rub	7		4	4.35	3.65		
Grain combines	Th.pieces	50		40	50	40		48
Mainline steam locomotives	Th.pieces	1.577	1.577		1.255	1.025	9.65	0.654
Mainline electric locomotives	Th.pieces	0.227	0.227	0.205	0.205			0.194
Mainline freight cars	Th.pieces	41	41	32	28	24		34.4
Mainline passenger railroad cars	Th.pieces	2.87		2.8	2.05	1.8		1.772

179

TABLE 2 (*continued*)

Nomenclature	Measure	GP (6/50)	GS (6/50)	MF (6/50)	GP (1/51)	GS (1/51)	GP (6/51)	MF (6/51)	GP 8/51	Final-1952 (Congress)	Results GKS-1957
Oil equipment	Th.tons				140		152		150	159.09	
Chemical equipment	Th.tons						200		160	138.95	111.2
Pumps centrifugal	Th.pieces	90							85		
Pumps—piston	Th.pieces	23							13		
Excavators	Th.pieces	5	5.5						3.75		5.25
Bulldozers	Th.pieces	6.8	7						3.7		7.511
Graders	Th.pieces	3							2.4		1.014
Scrapers	Th.pieces	4	4.5						3.5		2.025
Spinning machines	Th.pieces	1,050			900		1,000		950		2,040
Looms	Th.pieces	30.5			30				25		16
Tug vessels, river	Th.HP	127.95					156.5		141		
Barges with engines	Th.tons	55					45		45		
Barges without engines	Th.tons	904.2			1,047.7		1,084		900.8		
Tug vessels, sea	Th.HP	96.65					61		61		
Ships, sea	Th.tons	324.75					137.5		123.5	337.88	
Ships, river	Th.tons	19.5			42.95		42.95		42.95		
Fishing ships	Th.HP	126.4							104.4	56.67	
Ammonia	Th.tons	970	1,240				1,030		930		
Soda ash	Th.tons	1,640	1,900		1,708	1,738	1,708		1,495	1,396.35	
Caustic soda	Th.tons	570	650		570	647	570		536	581.48	563.4
Sulfuric acid	Mln.tons		4.3						4.176		
Inorganic fertilizers	Th.tons	8,050	10,500		9,700	422	9,700		9,300	9,502.17	9,640
Ammonium nitrate	Mln.tons		1.9								
Superphosphate	Mln.tons		5								
KCl	Mln.tons		1.135								
Ammonium sulfate	Mln.tons		0.735								
Synthetic rubber	Th.tons	300	480		300		300		300	300.00	
Natural rubber	Th.tons						22		20		

Product	Unit									
Hauling of commercial timber	Mln.cbm	246	300	246	300	246		244	240.91	212.1
Lumber	Mln.cbm	34	90	60	80	60		62		75.6
Paper	Th.tons	1,840	2,300	1,845	2,117	1,845		1,755	1,743.06	1,862
Cellulose	Th.tons	1,900	2,100					1,810		
Cement	Mln.tons	20	20	23.5	25	25		25	22.45	22.5
Window glass	Mln.sqm	100	115	95				80	304.76	99.8
Construction brick	Mln.pieces	30	35	23		25		30	28,630.71	20.8
Soft roofing materials	Mln.sqm	395	395			510		460		503.5
Asbestos shingles	Mln.pieces	1,600	1,900	1,600	1,800	1,600		1,600	1,419.80	
Ginned cotton	Mln.tons			2.38	2.5	2.38	2.38	1.965		
Cotton textiles	Mln.meters	6,500	7,150	7,000	6,600	6,680	7,600	6,580	6,268.52	5,905
Woolen textiles	Mln.meters	220	240	220	190	245	300	240	236.92	252.3
Linen	Mln.meters	500	620	660	550	500		500		305.5
Silk textiles	Mln.meters	200	220	230	240	245		260		525.8
Artificial fiber	Th.tons	113	113	324		133		133		110.5
Leather footwear	Mln.pieces	350	370	365	300	375	850	350	315.41	274.3
Hosiery	Th.pieces	900	960	915		945		900		772.2
Meat	Th.tons	2,800	2,800	2,900		2,900		2,400	2,412.57	2,524
Fish	Th.tons	3,025	3,175	3,000		3,000		2,900	2,828.40	2,737
Butter	Th.tons	600	660	600		600		550	556.47	463
Vegetable oil	Th.tons	1,540	1,540	1,500	1,700	1,500		1,350	1,381.21	1,168
Sugar	Th.tons	4,300	4,300	4,500	4,700	4,500	4,850	4,200	4,476.65	3,419
Soap	Th.tons	1,460	1,560	1,425		1,425		1,200		1,077
Crude alcohol, food	Mln.dkl	70	70		76			75		
Flour (centralized resources)	Mln.tons		19	19		19.5	21.5	19.5		
Groats	Th.tons	1,600	2,000		2,000			1,700		
Petroleum, refinery	Mln.tons	59	59					60		
Benzine, aviation	Mln.tons	3.72	3.72					3.6		
Benzine, automobile	Mln.tons	13.79	13.79					11		
Kerosine	Mln.tons	8.61	8.61					6.5		
Diesel oil	Mln.tons	7.3	7.3					8.1		
Heating oil	Mln.tons	6.83	6					14.8		
Diesel lubricate	Mln.tons	0.36	0.417							
Ship-oil	Mln.tons	1.55						2.4		

181

TABLE 2 (continued)

Nomenclature	Measure	GP (6/50)	GS (6/50)	MF (6/50)	GP (1/51)	GS (1/51)	GP (6/51)	MF (6/51)	GP 8/51	Final-1952 (Congress)	Results GKS-1957
Aviation lubricate	Th.tons	260							350		
Gas from coal and oil shale	Bln.cbm		2.85								
Compressors	Th.pieces	40			50		50				
Compressors (40–100)	Th.pieces		0.7								
Tires	Mln.pieces		16.3								
Crosstie, large scale	Mln.pieces	75	85			84					
Standard homes	Mln.sqm		5.9								
Paperboard	Mln.tons		0.6								
Asbestos	Th.tons	600	600			690					
Pipes, asbestos	Th.km	15	15								
Pipes, sewerage	Th.tons	350	350			320					
Tiles, metlakha	Th.sqm	4,000	7,000		3,000	5,980	3,000				
Sorlime	Th.tons	8,000	10,000								
Gypsum	Th.tons	5,000	8,000								
Stationary oil drainage machines—Uralmash	Th.pieces	0.75	0.38								
Locomobiles	Th.pieces		14								
Locomobiles, high capacity	Th.pieces		1.2								
Equipment, crushing	Th.tons		40								
Engines, gas generators	Th.pieces		7								
Plywood	Mln.cbm	1.2	1.3		1.2		1.09				
Wood pulp	Mln.tons		0.86								
Press and forging machines	Th.pieces	12.16	12.465			12.465			10.3		19.4

NOTE: GP = Gosplan; GS = Gossnab; MF = Ministry of Finance.

182

investment over the five-year period, all expressed in different prices of 1950 (January 1 and July 1). Other figures that are aggregated in money terms were trade turnover, economies from the lowering of production costs, average annual wages, and the wage fund. The reduction in production costs of industry and labor productivity growth were given in percentage terms, and two labor targets—the total number of workers and employees and the number of students—were also given. Gosplan also provided breakdowns of investment for 52 agencies expressed in constant 1950 prices. Gosplan's defense department provided very detailed defense equipment plans for the five-year period (under the label of completely secret, special importance), broken down for each year of the five-year period for 100 defense products and supplies in physical units. Thus the defense budget listed almost as many products in physical units as did the Gosplan plan for the entire economy. Gosplan's defense budgets also gave monetary aggregates for spending broken down into seven product categories. That there are no recorded discussions of the defense plan by other agencies suggests that it was prepared only by Gosplan for Politburo approval. Various defense plans are presented in Table 3.

The narrative to the Gosplan documents lays out the various directives that the plan is supposed to fulfill. The main targets were the growth of industry (at 12 percent per year), with heavy industry growing at 13 percent and light industry at 11 percent. The plan also gives growth rates for 30 products in physical units ranging from iron and coal to vegetable oil and fish. Capital investment in the Fifth Five-Year Plan was set at double that of the Fourth Five-Year Plan. National income should increase by 60 percent, retail prices should fall by 35 percent, capital investment in housing should double, and so on. Gosplan's 1952 narrative report required 26 pages to cover these priorities, ranging from the most general targets to specific construction projects.

With the exceptions of investment funds to be allocated to specific agencies and the quite detailed defense equipment and

TABLE 3
DEFENSE PLANS, FIFTH FIVE-YEAR PLAN:
MILITARY EQUIPMENT SUPPLY FOR 1951–1955

Draft of Jan. 23, 1950, Min. Rub. Prices 1950

	1950 (results)	1951	1952	1953	1954	1955	Total
Aviation	8750	13600	16000	18000	19500	20500	87600
Weapons	2380	3780	5210	6900	8510	9280	33680
Navy (ship construction)	5340	6230	7930	9230	10860	12400	46650
Ammunition	2550	4640	6400	7600	9600	10500	38740
Armored technics	1110	2120	3710	5190	6760	7910	25690
Military-technical equipment	2270	4020	4900	5980	7220	8340	30460
—Radiolocation technics	1100						
Total	24120	36940	47200	56800	66860	74100	281900

Source: 2.2591 (592-1-17)

Draft—1951 (no date available), Min. Rub. Prices Jan. 1, 1951

	1951	1952	1953	1954	1955	Total
Aviation	11000	15000	16530	16700	17310	76540
Weapons	3000	4450	5980	7330	8070	28830
Navy (ship construction)	6450	8200	9450	11350	12780	48230
Ammunition	3990	5660	6770	8630	9460	34510
Armored technics	1460	2320	3870	4660	5060	17370
Military-technical equipment	4000	4800	5600	6900	8000	29300
—Radiolocation technics	1940	4370	6890	8970	11300	33470
Total	32920	43160	51600	60260	66560	254500

Source: 2.2591 (592-1-18)

Explosives (000 tons)

	1951	1952	1953	1954	1955	1956
Gunpowder	183	225	n.a.	n.a.	n.a.	315–575
TNT	130	225	n.a.	n.a.	n.a.	259–290

Source: 2.2591 (592-1-17, 18)

TABLE 3 (continued)

Equipment Plan—Jan. 23, 1950

	50 Report	1951	1952	1953	1954	1955	Five-year
Aviation							
Planes-total	3954	6800	8360	8805	9230	9600	42795
Fighters	2281	3770	4280	4280	4280	4290	20900
jet fighters	2125	3490	4000	4000	4000	4010	19500
training fighters	56	600	600	600	600	600	3000
Bombers	480	910	1320	1420	1420	1420	6490
jet bombers	156	390	700	800	800	800	3490
heavy with piston engines	312	420	420	420	420	420	2100
training bombers	8	100	100	150	200	200	750
Transport planes	301	300	350	400	450	500	2000
Aircraft engines	14063	19070	21550	25230	26100	27110	119060
jet engines	4973	8670	12310	15210	16330	17300	69820
Weapons							
Antiaircraft artillery	882	1600	2418	3460	4300	4700	16478
Antitank artillery		100	200	400	600	700	2000
Troops artillery	2617	2024	2310	2805	2134	1230	10503
Machines guns and automatic carbines, Th.p.	454.6	650	850	1050	1050	1050	4650
Cartridges, 7.62 mm, Mln.p.	1050	1390.5	1495.5	1496.5	1546.5	1546.5	7475.5
Cartridges, 12.7–14.5 mm, Mln.p.	23.6	23.4	39	41	41	46	190.4
Armored weaponry							
Tanks, heavy			340	475	550	635	2000
Tanks, medium	1000	1600	2500	3200	3300	3300	13900
Tanks, amphibious		180	450	650	800	880	2960
Ammunition, Th.pieces							
Aviation shells	10225.2	20050	26700	34450	41600	48850	171650
Artillery shells							
37–57 mm	684.4	2200	2680	3430	4190	4800	17300
85–152 mm	3681.6	5533	7265	7735	8740	9982	39255
203–280 mm	5	2	2.5	2.5	2.5	3	12.5
Mines 160–240 mm	8	110	220	330	340	380	1380
Grenades, PG-2 and PG-82	360	1050	1400	1600	2200	2600	8850
Demolition aviabombs	37.4	57.9	96	142	207	268	770.9
Navy shells							
25–45 mm		101	624	1054	1454	1637	4870
100–152 mm	17.1	132.5	453.5	587	703	743	2619
305–406 mm		0.4	1.737	3.4	3.746	3.834	13.117

Source: 2.2591 (592-1-17, 1-6)

TABLE 3 (*continued*)

Plan 1951

		1951	1952	1953	1954	1955	Five-year
Aviation							
Planes-total		7260	9510	9525	8250	8855	43400
Fighters		4055	5000	5000	3300	3545	20900
jet fighters		3875	4800	4800	3100	3345	19920
training fighters		500	600	600	600	600	2900
Bombers		910	1400	1420	1420	1420	6570
jet bombers		390	700	800	800	800	3490
heavy with piston engines		420	420	420	420	420	2100
training bombers		100	100	150	200	200	750
Transport planes		300	350	400	450	500	2000
Aircraft engines		19530	22000	25230	26100	27110	119970
jet engines		9130	12800	15210	16330	17300	70770
Weapons							
Antiaircraft artillery	882	1600	2418	3460	4300	4700	16478
Antitank artillery		100	200	400	600	700	2000
Troops artillery	2617	2024	2310	2805	2134	1230	10503
Machines guns and automatic carbines, Th.p.	454.6	650	850	1050	1050	1050	4650
Cartridges, 7.62 mm, Mln.p.	1050	1390.5	1495.5	1496.5	1546.5	1546.5	7475.5
Cartridges, 12.7–14.5 mm, Mln.p.	23.6	23.4	39	41	41	46	190.4
Armored weaponry							
Tanks, heavy		—	100	450	700	757	2007
Tanks, medium		1600	2200	3200	3300	3300	13600
Tanks, amphibious		180	500	900	1100	1220	3900
Ammunition, Th.pieces							
Aviation shells		22040	31900	34300	40900	48700	177840
Artillery shells							
37–57 mm		2750	3820	3900	4190	4800	19460
85–152 mm		5576	7226	7692	8740	9982	39216
203–280 mm		3.6	3.5	4.5	4.5	5	21.1
Mines 160–240 mm		110	220	330	340	380	1380
Grenades, PG-2 and PG-82		1050	1500	1600	2200	2600	8950
Demolition aviabombs		62.7	96.6	138	207	268	772.3
Navy shells							
25–45 mm		101	1370	1400	1500	1600	5971
100–152 mm		135.5	207	300	400	500	1542.5
305–406 mm		0.4	1.6	3.4	3.7	3.9	13

Source: 2.2591 (592-1-18), P.241–247

supplies budget, the Gosplan plan was not an operational plan. Even its targets in physical units were too highly aggregated (only three types of metal products, one type of coal, metallurgical equipment, numbers of tractors, and so on). It was a long distance between such Gosplan plans and actual production operations.

Gossnab

Whereas Gosplan's task was to spell out the production tasks of the economy in general terms and to distribute investment among agencies, Gossnab's job was to ensure that the economy had adequate supplies to meet its production targets. Thus, Gossnab served as the representative of industrial users. As such, Gossnab sought to identify and to prevent bottlenecks and other disproportions.

Gossnab, therefore, looked carefully at Gosplan's production figures to ensure that they provided sufficient production to meet the material input needs of the economy's producers. Because Gossnab's job was to prepare a supply plan for industrial users, it criticized Gosplan for "routine work" that did not address the main problems of the five-year period. Gossnab routinely complained that Gosplan's plans preserved deficits of material inputs and equipment, did not consider interindustry balances, and were indifferent to the problem of building up the substantial reserves for production emergencies that Gossnab favored.[31] Moreover, Gossnab complained that Gosplan did not pay enough attention to cost economies, which would allow investment rubles to stretch further, and did not properly calculate the increased output that could be expected from capital investment.

Whereas Gosplan limited its "assortment" to 127 products, Gossnab worked with 169 product categories (see Table 2). The greater number of categories is explained both by the finer breakdowns of products (different types of steel) and by the absence of

---

31. Gossnab argued for what appears to be enormous reserves, such as a two-to-three-year reserve of nonferrous metals (p. 12).

some products from Gosplan's plans. Gossnab plans tended to be longer and contained the key "balances" of the economy— specialist calculations of product supplies (including imports) and industrial uses for these products. Gossnab prepared 55 balances, each signed by the appropriate department head, broken down by years of the five-year plan to show that balances could be achieved only if the (generally higher) Gossnab production figures were used.

In its drafts, Gossnab argued for more investment, more production, greater cost economies, more product assortment, and greater attention to quality. Gossnab pointed out to Stalin what it perceived to be a number of disporportions in the Gosplan draft: For example, it showed that under the Gosplan variants, there would not be enough steel production to meet the needs of machine building and capital investment.

The Ministry of Finance

The Ministry of Finance's job was to make sure that the economy produced sufficient tax revenues to pay the government's bills without printing money. Insofar as the two major revenue sources were profits taxes and turnover taxes on consumer goods, the Ministry of Finance lobbied for more consumer goods, whose sale generated turnover taxes; higher labor productivity, which lowered costs of production; and more economical use of resources, which also lowered costs of production. Lower costs of production benefited the Ministry of Finance by raising enterprise profits and raising turnover tax revenues (which were the difference between retail prices and wholesale prices). Consider the finance ministry's criticisms of Gosplan's draft: "Gosplan did not consider all possibilites to increase national income, raise labor productivity, and lower production costs and, in connection with this, understated the volume of national income and national consumption." More specifically, the Ministry of Finance criticized Gosplan's projections for labor productivity growth as being too low by historical standards, in spite of the fact that in the current plan are "broad measures for the industrialization of construction and the mechanization of construction work." Moreover, the Ministry of Finance felt that costs could be lowered 22 percent versus Gosplan's 15 percent figure. The Ministry of Finance also pointed out that Gosplan had underestimated the growth possibilities of cotton and linen, leather products, and silk—consumer goods that could be sold to generate sales tax revenues.

The Ministry of Finance's criticisms are contained in only seven printed pages; Gossnab's take about 100. Judging from his marginal notes, Stalin paid much closer attention to the finance ministry's comments than to those of Gossnab.

Gosplan's Defense

Gosplan defended its calculations quite vigorously, primarily from the criticisms of its rival Gossnab.[32] In its 25-page single-spaced response, Gosplan rejected virtually all of Gossnab's objections and recommendations, beginning with what it regarded as Gossnab's most serious complaints: that is, in arguing against Gossnab's proposal to significantly raise ferrous metals production, Gosplan pointed out that its lower target would not create the disproportions against which Gossnab warned, and suggested that Gossnab did not know what it was doing. According to Gosplan's calculations, its rate of growth of ferrous metals was sufficient to meet the needs of construction because Gossnab was using the wrong construction figure, and to meet the needs of machine building, which Gosplan argued would be producing more precision instruments that require less steel. Moreover, if Gossnab's proposal to increase ferrous metals production were accepted, capital investment for ferrous metals would have to be increased by 30 percent—a sum not available in the budget. Gos-

---

32. See, e.g., "O zakliuchenniiakh Gossnaba, Gostekhniki, Gosstroiia i TsU po proekty direktiv k sostavleniiu piatiletnogo plana razvitiia narodnogo khoziaistva SSSR na 1951–1995 gody," June 8, 1950 (592/1/14).

plan's defense of its plans was unrelenting: "Gossnab does not understand what it is doing; if we accept Gossnab's suggestions there have to be substantial increases in investment, etc." Gosplan also attacked Gossnab's demands for additional reserves: "The proposal of Gossnab to increase the production of bricks to 35 billion will result in the creation of unnecessary reserves of 5 billion bricks. In addition, one must consider that in order to meet Gossnab's proposal, it would be necessary to build an additional 595 concrete slab-block factories with a capacity of 6 million and 20 new brick factories every year, requiring an additional capital investment of more than one billion rubles." Gosplan also gave a strong defense of its own balances, such as the coal balance, saying that it had constructed them to yield balances of supplies and demands.

The remarkable feature of the Gosplan defense is that it rejected all Gossnab's proposals and stubbornly stuck with its own, even though Gossnab worked at a greater level of detail. If our interpretation of marginal marks is correct—that they were made by Stalin—Stalin reviewed Gosplan's defense of its own figures with care and made no corrections. It is noteworthy that Gosplan did not attack the Ministry of Finance's memos. Its "defensive critiques" were aimed at Gossnab.

CONCLUSIONS

The Soviet Union waited thirteen years for a new course to be set by Stalin's designated successors for the postwar era—though Stalin's designated successors were not entirely free to choose this course. Stalin, in spite of growing infirmity and loosening of control over his associates, remained the ultimate arbiter. The XIX Party Congress did indeed provide a venue for announcing the course of postwar Soviet policy. For those who expected something different, the XIX Party Congress was clearly a disappointment. Malenkov's keynote speech touched upon peaceful coexistence, greater party democracy, and criticism of economic performance, but it offerred no real solution to the economic deficiencies of the economic system that were already apparent in the early 1930s. There was no discussion of real economic reform, as there had been in the early 1930s (see chapter by Davies). The economy could now be criticized without blaming wreckers, but Malenkov and his associates did not propose alternatives to the problematic planning system that had been created some twenty years earlier.

The XIX Party Congress's major agenda item—approval of the Fifth Five-Year Plan—turned out to be a rather meaningless gesture. The Fifth Five-Year Plan had been formulated and basically completed before the party congress was even called. It was the product of technical debates among planning agencies. Nowhere in this debate was the issue of fundamental changes in priorities and procedures raised. The Fifth Five-Year Plan simply parroted the procedures of the fourth and earlier five-year plans. The archives provide no evidence of strong interest by Stalin, in contrast to his intense interest in five-year plans during the 1930s. He may have come to the conclusion that five-year plans were a hollow exercise.

The Hoover file on the XIX Party Congress, including the preparation of the Fifth Five-Year Plan, provides a behind-the-scenes glimpse of high-level decision making. It even supplies a detailed defense plan, which would have been regarded as a treasure trove by earlier Western researchers. The XIX Party Congress file reveals how five-year plans were constructed, who the participants were, and how outcomes were decided. One surprising feature is that the five-year plan was put together by the technical planning agencies, Gosplan, Gossnab, and the Ministry of Finance, with no official input from those who had to fulfill the plan; namely, the industrial ministries and regional authorities. Any process that lacks input from the eventual executors would be lacking in credibility. The new national supply agency, Gossnab, was not really a representative of industrial consumers; its sole concern was putting together a national supply plan that it could claim was balanced between supplies and demands. From the documents, it appears that it constructed its balances mathematically through scientific norms, not through communications with producers.

The Soviet Union, therefore, entered the postwar era much as it ended in 1991, tied to an economic system that had serious problems, whose operations had become routine, each with few ideas as to how to fix it.

INDEX